Freedom!

Freedom!

ESCAPING THE PRISON OF THE MIND

Ozay Rinpoche

Eremitical Press

POINT ROBERTS, WASHINGTON

Freedom! Escaping the Prison of the Mind
Copyright © 2008 Ozay Rinpoche
First Edition
Eremitical Press
Cover photographs by Ahiranta
Book design by Derek Cameron
Set in Adobe Caslon Pro 12/15 pt
Logo design by Peri Poloni-Gabriel

To contact the author write *abc_enlightenment@hotmail.com*

ISBN-10 0980081726
ISBN-13 978-0980081725
Library of Congress Control Number 2008920843

10 9 8 7 6 5 4 3 2 1

TO THE MEMORY of my courageous, unique, and beloved wife, Kaye, who was taken from us by that vile disease of mankind, cancer.

As I walked through the forest of life in search of peace, love, and happiness, I came to a clearing where sunlight filtered through the shade and all wondrous things grew. In the midst of the clearing I spotted a flower of many colors and of beauty untold. I was drawn to its splendor and grace; I was humbled in its presence.

My instinct was to pluck the flower so that I could call it mine. "But how could I, so lowly as I am, own such a treasure?" my inner voice said. And so I let it be, bathed in the warmth of the sun, and simply stood by its beauty without moving from its side.

I closed my eyes in sleep. How lucky was I to have stumbled upon such a precious gift! How could I deserve this, after all the bad things I had done? How could I be worthy?

Sixteen years passed, and one day I opened my eyes and the flower was no more. It had perished.

Again and again, I closed my eyes, twice in heart-felt grief, and once in understanding. The first time I saw death, and all that goes with it; the second, I saw union with the great Mother Earth, and the feeling of loss, and the holding on; and the third, I saw rebirth, and a new life, and a new beginning. For what dies is born again: the caterpillar becomes the beautiful butterfly. Where once stood that single beauty now stood seven others. It was then that I was given understanding.

Until the time our souls meet in the next life (love is now and for eternity), rest in peace, my sweet love, and be renewed.

KAYE

OCTOBER 4, 1953–OCTOBER 27, 1998

Contents

Preface　*ix*

1　Childhood Memories　1

2　Boxing　21

3　Out to Sea　27

4　Back Home　37

5　In the Army　45

6　Absent without Leave　65

7　Giving Up　77

8　Learning to Meditate　103

9　Dreams　129

10　The Material World　137

11　Out of Prison　141

Epilogue　*159*

APPENDIX A　*Meditation*　*165*

APPENDIX B　*Dream Interpretation*　*171*

Preface

WHAT I OFFER you in this book is freedom. Most people unknowingly live their lives in a prison. I will take you on a guided tour of the realms of imprisonment. If your enthusiasm is strong enough, you will be able to realize this freedom for yourself, and taste the joy that is available to those who are willing to do the work.

Ask yourself how often you wake up in the morning feeling excited about something—the next pay packet, the next party, the next vehicle, the next romantic partner—only to discover that things never quite work out the way you expect?

The one certainty is that you will continue to believe that satisfaction exists somewhere in the future. With repeated disappointments, your motivation and energy may fail. Even the will to live can be lost.

There is a better alternative.

The disciples often asked Jesus about the kingdom of heaven. Once Jesus called a child into their midst and told them that to enter the kingdom of heaven, they must "become as little children" (Matthew 18:3).

When we become as children, all things in life take on new meaning, and we see through the eye of a child. Everything is fresh, and with this freshness enthusiasm returns. A whole new energy-cycle begins.

Freedom is about awakening from the great sleep. By sleep I mean the state of being captivated by the mechanical, unobserved mind—the unfocused mind, the mind that is like a boat without a rudder, driven by the wind. Even as you read these words, your mind may already be drifting off in different directions.

I would like to help you to know yourself, and become a self-realized or enlightened human being—if not fully, then at least on an intellectual level. A purely intellectual understanding can at least be the start of authentic development toward self-realization.

This book tells the story of my life. I do this not to promote myself, but to give you a tangible example of what self-realization means. Though superficially about me, at a deeper level the book is about you, since you are the one who must discover the truth for yourself.

As for my credentials, these were earned while I was serving a prison sentence, first in Cardiff prison in Wales, and then in Dartmoor prison in England. Through diligent work, I became enlightened.

Enlightenment means rising above the ego with its ideas and theories whose root is so often the desire to look good to others. This is a form of self-deceit, and the result of the workings of the lower nature. To feel peace—the great peace—you have to learn to read the book of Self. It is in that book that all the answers may be found. One has to learn to know the ego, and finally to conquer the ego.

The ego is the one who fights, who derives satisfaction from positions of power, and who revels in feelings of self-importance. You must learn to destroy this ego. Step back from the mind, and observe its workings. By so doing, you create the conditions necessary for the development of the higher mind—the mind that witnesses the workings of the lower, or thinking mind.

This thinking mind is not really your own. Rather, as you go through life, you identify with traits coming from outside of yourself. A trait may be something as simple as a gesture, an expression, or a point of view. You pick these up from your parents, from friends you admire, even from people you hate. You then incorporate these traits into yourself, and mistakenly identify with them. After a while, you think of these external characteristics as "I" or "me."

Having built such a prison, you must then protect it. This is the origin of the ego. The ego is the one who guards the fortress built from false identities. Whenever the edifice comes under attack, the ego will use whatever means available to defend it.

Rigidly-defended people may say: "Everyone is entitled to their own opinion." In reality, everyone is entitled to know the truth, and there is only one truth. The person you *think* you are is a pretender.

Do you ever find yourself lost in the sleep of the mind, and drawn away from the task at hand? Are you aware of those moments? If you can become aware, you will begin work of reaching true light and true peace. But this goal can be reached only through constant work on the self.

Keep watching your mind. Learn to know yourself. As you make the effort to learn, you will begin to know more and more, until eventually you will know the great peace and light. Then you will be among the seers, prophets, and sages of all ages. Apparent burdens take on new forms, and life becomes joyful and blissful. You are free.

This freedom has always been there, but fear of the unknown can make you hold on all the more tightly. If you have the courage to let go, you will see that life can be so much better, both for yourself, and for the people who are connected to you in life.

❈ *1* ❈

Childhood Memories

NOTHING IN MY early childhood suggested I would end up in prison. There was, though, one curious incident at the time of my birth.

On the day I was born, some student nurses were so impressed with what a handsome baby I was they took me away for the day. Nobody knows where they took me. My mother and father were worried, of course, until the nurses returned. Though I do say so myself, I'm still good-looking today!

When I reached eighteen months, my mother and father decided to take my older brother and sister and myself to live in the country, where we would have a back garden to play in. A war-time friend of my father's helped him find a house in a mining valley called Garndiffaith, which is just outside Pontypool, Wales.

After we moved in, my mother and father discovered the house was not what they had expected. It turned out to be a derelict miner's cottage in a bad state of disrepair. There was no hot water, no partitions between the bedrooms, and the toilet was outside. My mother's and father's first job was to shovel all the accumulated rubble out of the house.

Dad got a job, but six weeks after we moved in had a heart attack and passed away, may his soul rest in peace. Though I never got to know him, I feel as if he has always been close to me, especially during my times of need. I love him with all my heart.

I was close, too, to my big sister, Margerate, who would eventually pass away at the young age of fifty-one. She went to bed one day and never woke up. When she died, it brought back a memory of a conversation I had with her when we were young.

We sat in the little room with the coal fire burning. It was cold outside, and nearing time to go to bed. Margerate mentioned that every night she went to bed, she would recite a prayer to protect herself in the event she died in her sleep.

This aroused my curiosity. Being so young, I did not know one could die in one's sleep. It scared me to think of such a thing happening, and not having any say in the matter.

Since Margerate's death, that incident has often come to mind, and I have frequently wondered if she had some premonition of it, or whether she may have lived before and experienced the same thing in a previous life. My big regret is that I never told her how much I loved and admired her—my "big sis."

I mention these deaths for two reasons: first, out of respect for these beloved members of our family, and second, because these painful life-experiences can make us into better people. Too many of us, I believe, do not give enough consideration to death and all that death implies.

Despite the fact that our house in the Garndiffaith (or "Garn," as the locals call it) was small, to me it was home and felt very comfortable. We would huddle around the coal fire and moan at anyone who took up the heat by standing immediately in front of the fire. In winter times especially, I would notice the front door had a wide gap underneath it. Through this gap snow would blow under the door and into the front room.

As I neared the age of three, my mother became concerned that

I had not yet spoken a single word. She took me to the doctor, who examined me, found me healthy, and told her I would learn to speak in my own time. This put my mother's mind at rest.

My first encounters with the spirit realm took place in that house in the Garn. Our home was undoubtedly haunted. I would lie in bed with my brother at the top end and me at bottom. Then I would hear noises such as banging and footsteps. Being the child I was, I would pretend they were birds and animals.

Quite often, I would wake in the morning to find one of my socks had gone missing. My mother gave me a hard time about this. She could not afford to keep replacing socks or other items of clothing, she told me.

Her scolding made me careful to put the socks where I thought they would not go missing. I believed at first it was mice who were taking them, but soon realized that mice would be unable to crawl under my pillow and remove socks without my knowing about it.

My mother did not believe that socks were disappearing from under my pillow. In the end I am sure she did know, but would not say so. One of her philosophies was that if you did not believe in something it would go away, whereas if you believed it then you made it real.

Once, as I was lying in bed, I heard what sounded like wind coming up the stairs and making a strange howling sound. I reacted by trying to imitate the sound myself. In hindsight, it is obvious that such a sound could not have occurred naturally in that part of the house. The stairs were completely isolated from any doors or windows.

If I ever lay on my back to go to sleep, I would feel as if I were being carried up and out of the house in a vortex of wind. This frightened the living daylights out of me, and I would sleep on my side to avoid the experience. Even today, I will always lie on my side rather than on my back.

As I got older, I took to sleeping under the blankets, since I was so frightened of the dark and of the supposed "ghost" my mother would threaten us with in order to make us get to bed promptly. But we had a ghost for real.

Once, I heard my name called out several times. Even after inspecting all possible sources for the voice, I could not find out who was responsible. Since my mother was downstairs on her own, I went to ask her if she was the one who had called me. As expected, the answer was no. It had not even sounded like her. The voice was that of a man, and in any case, I would have recognized my mother's voice.

I told her about this incident, but she put it down to my imagination. It was real, however—as real as my mother.

Later in life, my mother told me her own story of an incident in Garn. She was lying in bed one night when a misty figure appeared. After a while the figure became more solid. My mother recognized it as my father. He did not say anything to her, but was as real as I am. She told me that, although he had said nothing, she felt as if he wanted to check to see that she was alright.

I had a feeling that not only was I alive now, but that I had always been alive. However, it seemed important to me to confirm this belief with my mother. I was certain she was going to tell me what I already knew, but she said: "No. You only have one life to live, and one day you will die, and that will be the end of it."

Her answer left me depressed. Prior to that, I had a calm about me, because I was sure of my eternal existence. In one fell swoop it was taken away.

The impression that conversation made on me stayed with me for some time. After all, she was my mother, and at that age I thought my mother knew everything. Such is the innocence of the young child.

Shortly after this, I remembered a technique I had learned in a previous lifetime. I would ask a question and allow the answer to arise within me. I could not possibly have known this technique from any source other than a previous life, since at that time I had so little experience of this life.

When I remembered this technique, the great burden of death was lifted from me, and my previous calm returned.

One day I asked myself the question: What is the purpose of my life? What am I here for?

The answer came to me as if from the back of my head. I did not feel that it came from the everyday "I," but rather from a place deep within me. I was here to be a teacher, and to learn all the things that were new since the last appearance of my soul on earth.

Another time, I asked myself the question: Who am I? And what is this "I"?

It came to me that I could not possibly "be" the name my mother had given me, since this was just a name. So who was I? I am just this, this life. I am here, and I simply am.

As the years went by, I forgot these events, and lost that inner peace, until eventually it returned during my stay in prison. But that was still a long way in the future.

It was now time for me to go to school. Here I would inadvertently get into trouble.

THE DOORS OF my first school seemed huge to me. One day, I rushed through them too hastily. As I let the doors slam behind me, I heard a loud scream.

I turned to see a girl holding up her hand. Her little finger hung to one side, attached to the hand only by a sliver of skin. I stood and stared, utterly speechless. A dinner lady came and hurried the girl off.

Shortly after this, I was summoned to the Head Mistress's office and questioned about the incident. I explained exactly what I had done: I had slammed the door, and then I saw the little girl with the finger hanging off.

The Head Mistress did not seem to believe me. I could not understand why. Until that time I had believed it was normal to speak the truth, and therefore adults would always believe me.

She let me off with a caution, but for some time after this I was

5

puzzled by her behavior. The memory of our conversation darkened my mood whenever I thought about it.

In the early days at school I had only one friend, and spent most of my time on my own. Our class began to congregate around one particular child, John Macadam. He had an uncanny ability to inspire the other children to think of themselves as heroes.

In those days, the second world war was still constantly being discussed on television, and war with its accompanying killing and violence became focus of their heroism. All our schoolyard play focused on war. It is not surprising that our generation would eventually develop a reputation for gang warfare.

One young lad had the most curly hair you could ever imagine. Because he looked so different, the group of young world war two soldiers made this young lad's life a misery. I was tempted to befriend him, until I figured out that if I did so, I too would become their victim. After this, I thought it wise to keep myself to myself.

One day the gang began to pick on me anyway. Their target was often chosen randomly, and tended to be whichever child was on his own. My turn arrived. I was terrified as John Macadam approached me with his platoon of child-soldiers.

We spoke a few words that I do not remember. I was determined not to show my fear. At that point, I literally had my back against the wall. Then the fight started. It was me against the entire gang.

They began lashing out. I flailed back with no real aim as to where the punches would land. Suddenly, the fight was over, and John Macadam was clutching his nose, blood gushing from it. He must have caught one of the flurry of punches.

Without intending it, I now had a gang of my own. I was the hero who had stood up to the villain and come off the victor. From that time through to secondary school, life in the schoolyard was one never-ending battle for supremacy.

It was now several years since my father died. My mother was ready to get on with her life. She remarried, and had another two children—my younger brother and sister.

The marriage turned out to be a disaster. Her new husband was a womanizer, and he abused my older brother and sister. My brother still suffers from the after-effects of that abuse to this day.

We were still living in the Garn, and one morning I came downstairs to see urine and excreta all over the place, and my mother with two black eyes. All mother said was: "I hope next time I see him, he's sitting in a wheel chair."

After a few years of separation, the next time she saw him was in child support court. He was indeed in a wheel chair. This left him unable to work and earn money, and my mother was in an even worse situation than before. Instead of three children to raise on her own, she now had five.

Those were difficult days for my mother. What compounded her difficulties was the fact that she was a Greek-Cypriot immigrant, who had never had the opportunity to learn to read and write. At the time she was in school in Cyprus, the war was raging, and she had to leave school early to help build the roads needed for the war effort. Incredibly, she would only have been about eight years old at the time. She was, though, a very strong lady, and by today's standards she did the impossible.

Margerate was fourteen by now. Since our mother found it difficult to make ends meet, Margerate had to leave school and take a job to help support the family.

She was just getting to the time in her life when she wanted some fun and excitement, and I suppose the prospect of helping my mother raise us must have depressed her. After a couple of years, she ran away from home.

Margerate went to London, where so many teenage runaways find themselves. We heard nothing from her for two years. I missed her terribly, but would never say so.

My mother got the police involved, and eventually they found Margerate and told my mother she was safe and well. However, since she was now legally an adult, the police would not give us her address, and Margerate herself did not want our mother to know

7

where she was.

By this time, my mother had decided it was time for us to move. Almost anything seemed better than our run-down miner's house, and she moved us to a new housing project called Trevethin. There we had to start at a new school, Snatchwood.

Snatchwood was built next to a quarry face which was fenced off to prevent the children gaining access to it. The quarry did not bother me at first, but one day I had a vision of the whole thing collapsing, and burying all the children in the schoolyard under rocks. The vision made me so afraid I gave the entire area a wide berth.

About two weeks after my vision, there was a disaster at a place called Aberfan. A slag heap collapsed due to heavy rain, and over one hundred children were killed by falling slag.

Shortly after the disaster, all the slag heaps in Wales were leveled off, and our quarry face was covered with protective wire meshing. This relieved my fears.

I had another problem to deal with in my early days at my new school. Some of the children wanted to find out what I was all about. In any gathering of children or adults, often there emerges a need to test the new boy on the block to see if he is a threat, to push him down out of competition's way, and ultimately either to give him respect or to walk all over him.

There is, too, a primeval and unconscious instinct to find out who is the best fighter. Perhaps this is related to the desire for the group to have a leader, and for the leader to have as many followers as possible. The more followers you have, the more respect you get.

This urge to dominate can be found in most social groups, but it manifests in more sophisticated forms as we get older. Among adults, it crystallizes into such things as being the competitive businessman, or boasting of intelligence in subtle ways, or thinking oneself better than other people at some activity ("I have this, and this is special, and that makes me better").

The reality is that as God's creation we are all special, but this genuine "special-ness" is something not based on being better than other people. It is like the dog saying to the cat, "I am special, because I am a dog and you are a cat." This is where the enemy of mankind, the ego, is born. Without the ego, we would look at our fellow human beings and all forms of life on earth and be able to see them as our brothers and sisters.

Things being what they were, it was arranged I was going to have to fight to prove myself. We would all meet after school and settle the matter. There was no dispute, no fallout, nothing. It was just coldly accepted that it had to be done.

The boy I was to fight was named Pete Murphy.

AFTER SCHOOL WAS was over for the day, we met on the top of the hill we all had to climb on our way home. Just a bit further on was a wooded area with a clearing in which the fights were always held. All the children who were under no pressure from their parents to get home straight after school would stop to see the fight.

The fight began with a flurry of punches. I do not remember who threw the first punch, but we fought, and we fought, and we fought. It went on and on, until we were at a standstill on the ground with neither of us willing to give an inch to the other.

After what must have been an hour interlocked in battle, we were totally exhausted, but still not willing to give in. Our audience had dwindled to one curious little boy wearing glasses, shorts, and a school cap. After a while, even he disappeared.

The boy returned with his parents, who broke up the fight. From that day on, Pete Murphy and I became the closest of friends. Our friendship has lasted to this day.

Pete and I had a lot of adventures together, and became like brothers. We would play pranks, and were always dreaming up new schemes to get money to buy our favorite treats—custard cream cookies and sponge cakes.

When we were not doing this, we would be out bird-nesting. We each had a bird egg collection, and it was our pride and joy. The idea came from an uncle of Pete's, who had a birds' egg collection, and who arranged his eggs in an artistic display. Each egg had a story to go with it describing the adventure by which that particular egg had been collected.

Many a time we would find ourselves in all sorts of predicaments because of our enthusiasm for this hobby. We were only about seven years old when we started. At that time, nobody cared about such things as wildlife protection, and we did not know any better.

On one occasion, we decided we wanted to add a raven's egg to our collections. The ravens nested on a high quarry face that must have been at least seventy feet from top to bottom. All we had to do to get to them was to clamber across a rock face—with the seventy-foot drop below us.

Pete never showed any sense of danger, but when I looked at that quarry face it put the fear of God into me. I would never show this fear to anyone, of course, as I believed I had an image to maintain, and I was not going to let anyone see my fear.

We decided Pete would climb across the rock face first. I watched carefully where he put his hands and feet, so that I could copy his every movement when my turn came.

At one point he got into trouble. I looked at his predicament and hoped he would decide he could not do it, so that we could call the whole thing off. To my dismay, Pete somehow found a way across to the relative safety of a ledge on the far side of the difficult patch. The raven's nest was just a little further on.

After Pete got to the ledge, he stopped and called out to me: "Come on! I'll watch you across." Perhaps he sensed my fear, or perhaps he just knew it was a difficult climb. Neither of us would ever admit to any weakness.

My heart went to my mouth. I thought to myself: "I'll do it. If he can do it, then so can I." This was my rationalizing to overcome my fear. I had been sure Pete would turn back. Now he was calling for me. I had no choice. It was do or die.

I began to climb across the rock face, and got past the first part without much difficulty. Then I got to the area I knew was going to be a problem. A certain point would support the weight of only one leg, since one's full weight would cause the toehold to collapse. The other leg had to be stretched out at a seventy-degree angle. The only hand grips were small cracks in the rock face that allowed one or two inches of the fingers to be inserted.

Suddenly I froze with fear. Every muscle was rigid. Thoughts of falling from the rock face flooded my mind. I said to myself: "This is it. I'm going to die." With that, I froze even more rigidly.

Then I become aware of another thought-process in my mind. This was a more logical way of thinking that told me that the more afraid I became, the less chance I had of making it to safety. The best thing I could do would simply be to stay where I was, and hope that someone would call the fire department to come to my rescue.

I relaxed momentarily. But then I encountered another problem. Due to all this continual exertion, my hands and legs were beginning to give me tremendous pain.

Something had to be done soon. If the fire department was going to come, Pete would have to be the one to alert them. Since he would have had to pass by me to do so, this was now impossible. It was all up to me.

The thought of just staying there out of fear was so strong, and so easy to give into. In the end, I concluded that if I did not do something soon, I was going to fall to my death.

I looked at what I had to do. Pete was encouraging me, telling me where to place each foot and hand in turn. I did not like the idea of holding on with only one hand, but knew I had to momentarily do so in order to make progress. It was my only chance.

When I reached the ledge, my heart was pounding so hard I could hear it thudding. The next few steps were easier. I got to where Pete was, and at last felt safe. I took a deep breath, still trembling from what I had been through.

We decided to continue on to the raven's nest. Pete went first.

When he came back, he said there were no eggs in the nest anyway. So we sat on the ledge and chatted for a while.

Then I realized that to get home, we could have to make the dangerous crossing once more.

MY MUSCLES STILL ached from the first crossing. I needed time to recover before I was ready to go through the same thing again. I was not looking forward to it.

The time came, and we decided to go back. Again, I carefully watched Pete's movements. Though he had some difficulty, he got across the quarry face relatively easily.

As he was climbing back, I wondered how he managed to make it look so easy. *Perhaps he is not smart enough to realize how dangerous it is*, I thought. Then I wondered if it could be because he was shorter than me. But that could not be the answer, since being smaller, he had to jump proportionately further. Yet he seemed to do it effortlessly.

My mind churned out excuses as to why Pete had no problem, while for me it was incredibly difficult. Finally, I came to the conclusion that the problem was I was thinking about the whole thing too much, while Pete was not. Even before we decided to start this expedition, I was the one to say: "Hang on. Let's plan how we're going to do this climb. Look at the rock face. We will do this, and then we will do that with the other foot," and so on.

Pete had just wanted to get on with it without any thoughts or plan of attack, relying solely on instinct. My mind, on the other hand, was thinking of all the possibilities, and all the different angles. All my energy went into formulating ideas.

A light went on. I realized it was my thinking mind that was stopping me. It was my mind that had stirred up all my fear! Thought alone prevented me from traversing the rock face without problems.

That mind could so easily have cost me my life!

When I came to this conclusion, I made a resolution to focus totally on the rock face, and not think about the possibility of falling, nor of how high off the ground we were.

It came to my turn to go back across.

I could see the look on Pete's face. It was as if he knew I was going to have a problem. He would shout out advice as to where to put my feet. I knew I did not want to feel that fear again, so I blocked all thoughts from my mind, except thoughts as to how to cross the rock face. My concentration was focused solely on my hands and feet, and on where I was going to put them next.

Before I knew it, what I had deemed to be a threat to my life was over and done with.

This little escapade taught me a truth in life at an early age. The mind can be useful, but it can also be debilitating when used in the wrong way.

Pete and I went on to have many more such adventures. We were always up to some mischief or another.

Once we took on the task of going door-to-door to collect money for a Royal Air Force charity. Each of us had a tray of little pins in the shape of R.A.F. wings to give out in exchange for donations.

We decided this would be a good way to make a bit of cash for ourselves, so we could buy our favorite custard creams and sponge cake.

First, we went round all the houses in our own neighborhood. Even after doing this, we still found we had too many wings left. Our thinking was that the more we sold, the more money we would have for ourselves.

Then we came up with the idea that collecting in a wealthier neighborhood would result in larger donations. Our theory turned out to be correct.

We covered many miles, but our feet but did not seem to mind, and we would stop every once in a while to empty out the collection box to see how much we had collected. This was easy to do. Simply turning the box upside down and inserting an ice pop stick in the slot allowed the coins to roll out.

With each success, we became all the more enthusiastic. Even when it began to rain, we carried on, despite the fact we were both now tired and exhausted, and the weather was becoming increasingly cold and windy.

After trudging through the rain for a couple of hours, we went back to Pete's place, and emptied out the collection box.

When we counted it, we had collected over twenty pounds, a huge sum of money. We decided to remove three pounds each as our "commission" for the collecting work. In the following days the temptation to remove even more became too strong, and we made a total of three withdrawals, removing altogether fifteen pounds and leaving only five.

The day came for us to take the collection box back to school. I was not looking forward to it. In a vain attempt to avoid the inevitable, I decided to become ill, and gave the collection box and my empty tray to Pete to take back to school.

I was sure he would be in the deep end, and when it was time for me to go back to school, I would be in trouble too.

The next day, I saw Pete and waited for him to tell me what the teachers had said, and what trouble he was in. He did not mention the subject. I thought he had forgotten, or else that he just did not want to mention it for some reason.

Eventually, I had to go back to school, since it had become impossible for me to take any more time off. All my excuses had run out.

In the hallway, I saw the teacher who was in charge of the collection, and pretended not to notice him. This charade continued for several days. I came to the conclusion they had not yet counted the money.

Then, one morning, we were in school assembly, and they said that next day they would have an announcement to make about the R.A.F. collection. The morning the announcement was due, I made a lot of trips to the washroom! Here I was, and this was going to be it.

I stood in morning assembly ready for the worst. Only a week before, the headmaster had my brother up on the stage to cane him because he was in trouble for fighting. I was sure that this week it was going to be my turn.

The headmaster started to read out the names of the pupils who had collected money. With each set of names, he would state how much money they had collected. The amounts ranged from ten shillings to about three pounds. This sounded good, I thought. But then how could it be explained that we had sold a full tray of pins, and not handed over more than five pounds? Even if you received a penny for each pin, you would still have more than five pounds.

As the headmaster reached Pete's and my name, I felt a sense of foreboding. My legs began to shake. My mind raced to prepare an excuse. Perhaps we could say we lost the pins, or that some big bullies came and took almost all the money, leaving us with only five pounds.

The headmaster said: "And now I want the whole school to give a round of applause for the team that has collected the most."

It was us!

I was so pleased. If only they had known the truth!

The incident made me aware how temptation can be stronger than common sense. I did not want to put myself in that position ever again—or so I thought at the time. As you will see, one sometimes forgets life's lessons.

When we got to secondary school, we began to play truant. This became a regular habit, especially at times when we had academic subjects such as English or geography. I never skipped classes that involved using my artistic skills or making things, though.

We would either go to someone's house or, if the weather was warm, climb the trees opposite the school and taunt the children who were still in the schoolyard.

Once, someone who owned a ball-bearing repeater air rifle decided to shoot at the children in the schoolyard. This was extreme, even by our standards, and the school called the police to come and keep an eye on the area. Such was the uncontrollability of the teenagers around that part of Wales at the time.

IT WAS WHILE playing in the trees one day that we witnessed a phenomenon I cannot explain even to this day.

On that particularly day there was Pete Murphy, Steve Wells, and myself. We were playing among the trees on the grounds of a graveyard that was overgrown with grass, weeds and bushes. A couple of weeks earlier, Steve Wells's grandfather had been buried in that same graveyard, not far from where we were playing. Before climbing the trees, we went to see his grave.

When we were up the tree, I noticed something strange emerging from among the brambles. To get a closer look, I came down from the trees. The closer I got, the more mystified and frightened I became.

It looked like a cloud of concentrated steam, about three feet in diameter. It was rising out of the solid earth.

I shouted to Pete and Steve to come and see. They, too, got down from the trees, and came to have a look. All of a sudden, the three of us bolted like lightning.

The only description I can give you is that it was like a genie who had just come out of a bottle. I have never seen anything like that before or since, and to this day I am mystified as to what it was. It was certainly not my imagination, as all three of us saw the same thing.

When we grew into teenagers, we began to go to discos. One of the best was at a place called Court Bleddyn. All the "talent" would go there once a week. Since we were young and full of hormones, it was a must.

Court Bleddyn was out in the country some distance away from us. Being young lads in school, we had neither our own transportation, nor the money to pay for a taxi. Sometimes we managed to talk one of the older ones into giving us a ride in their vehicle. Even if we were lucky enough to get a ride there, usually we had to make our own way back.

On one such night, Pete and I had been to Court Bleddyn, and we were walking the ten miles back home. Our route took us through mostly unlit roads and pitch-black countryside. A young couple followed behind us.

Because it was so dark, we could not see who they were. We could hear them laughing and giggling, though. Then we heard them having some kind of discussion.

Eventually, we came to a stretch where the road was long and straight, and lit by occasional streetlights. Out of curiosity, we turned to see who this couple was. We could still hear them talking. But when we looked back, there was no one there.

We walked on, then looked back again. The couple sounded as if they were very close. The lit part of the road now stretched back for some distance, much further than our hearing range. We had heard them following us for some time. But, again, there was no one there. It spooked us so much, we ran from the spot as if we were powered by rocket fuel.

Prior to this, we had another mysterious experience on that same stretch of road. We were on a part that was almost pitch black, with high hedges on both sides. It was the hedges that made it so dark. On clear stretches the moonlight made for good visibility.

As we entered a particularly dark patch, we heard what sounded like electrically-generated noise, similar to the sound you hear when you stand near electricity pylons. This noise followed us for some distance.

We realized the sound could not be coming from anything stationary, as it followed us everywhere we traveled. When we got to a part of the road where the hedges were lower, we decided to look behind the hedges to see what this sound was.

We climbed over a gate, and to our surprise could not find anything to explain the noise that had followed us for so many miles. To this day, this remains another unsolved mystery.

On talking to people about the incident with the couple, we

discovered that, some time before, a young couple had been knocked down on that patch of road and killed outright.

I could well believe that, because it was out in the country, the road was narrow, and you needed to have your wits about you. No one in a car would expect to see you there at that time of night. I gathered from this that we must have encountered the spirits of the young couple who had been killed in an accident.

If any one is interested in this type of phenomenon, and would like to know where these incidents took place, it is the road from Court Bleddyn to Little Mill, just outside Pontypool. Try it in the early hours of the morning and see. Be careful, though, because that road is dangerous! Both times I walked it, there were strange phenomena, and I would say the chances are you would experience something, too.

Neither Pete nor I were very interested in what school had to offer academically, and Pete even less so than me. Because I was in the "B" stream and he was in the "C" stream, we did not see so much of each other at that time.

When I did see Pete one day, he told me he had started down at Jack Evans' Boxing Club in Pontynewynydd. I was not interested in boxing, except for Mohammed Ali's fights. Though he was one of my sport heroes, I thought boxing was not for me personally.

Pete did ask if I wanted to go, but I told him, "No, I'm not interested." I had started taking judo classes, and thought this was better.

Judo never mustered the respect that boxing did, though, and Pete reminded me of this. Again, he asked me to go with him.

I did not like the idea of being hurt, and I did not want to get up in that ring and have people see me getting beat. There was no way was I going to risk damaging my image as the toughest.

Finally, Pete said: "I only go down there to keep fit. That's all I do it for." I thought this was a good idea, so I went with him.

It was an impressive set-up. There were punch bags, reflex balls, speed balls, weights, heavy leather balls, and all over the walls were pictures of old boxers of bygone days. They had a ring, of course, and the entire Welsh boxing squad trained in that gym. They also had a few European champions, who to me at that age looked quite scary.

It turned out that I enjoyed the training. For a number of weeks, though, I managed to avoid the sparring. There was no way I was going get in that ring. I had watched people sparring, and seen the blood and mucus flying out of the ring. One day I saw someone getting knocked out, and that put me off even more.

My excuses kept me out of the ring for four weeks, but it was inevitable that eventually I would either have to get in the ring, or stop training. Jack Evans was only interested in spending his time and effort on motivated boxers.

So there I was. No more excuses.

As old Ernie Morgan gloved me up, puffing on his Woodbine cigarettes that made my eyes water, I could feel my mouth getting dry, and a sickly feeling in my stomach. Before I got in the ring, I vomited over his shoes.

My heart told me to stop, to call it a day, and not to train any more. The problem was, half a dozen of the lads from school were watching. Their eyes were on me—the one who had worked so hard to maintain a reputation of being the hardest individual around.

This was my day of reckoning. I would be shown up for what I really was.

I had no choice but to get in the ring and spar.

2

Boxing

I WAS TO fight a lad who had been boxing for a while. I glared at him, and before we even got in the ring, I already had him psyched out. I was good at this. In his eyes I could see a weakness, and I was going to use that weakness to get the better of him.

The rest was easy. It was a matter of creating within me the right act to play on his weakness.

After old Ernie gloved me up (and choked me with his cigarette fumes), I was ready.

As we started to spar, I could feel the lads from school watching my every move. We were the tough crowd, and no one from anywhere around here was better than us. I was defending not only my own reputation, but also theirs.

My opponent had been boxing since he was seven or eight, and he was good on his feet. He would jab, then move away whenever I got close to him. I sensed the fear that lay behind this approach.

Now I had to do something about it. I decided that for every hard punch I received, I would give him two hard ones back.

This strategy turned out to be a winner.

To my surprise, over the next few months I started to enjoy the sparring. I began to spar with everyone, from bantamweights all the way through to heavyweights. Sparring gave me a feeling of power I enjoyed, and earned me respect. I felt in complete control.

The only thing I did not like was having to box in front of audiences. Spectators made me nervous, though in time I would overcome this.

In the ring, no one could get near me. I had quickly mastered the craft, and I knew it. One of my brother's friends asked Jack Evans if he thought I was any good at boxing. Jack, who was quite an authority on boxing at that time, told him I was another John Conteh.

When I was told about this, I felt insulted. I thought I was much better than John Conteh. If he had said Mohammed Ali, I might have been happier about the whole affair—such was the arrogance of my ego.

This ego was being fed all the time by my friends, and every fight provided it with more food. Boxing became an addiction that took priority over everything else. My aim was to become world champion, and to be better than any other boxer who had ever lived.

When I trained, I made sure I trained harder than anyone else in the gym, and always did more, or did the same thing faster. I was highly competitive. The only thing that gave me satisfaction was doing better than anyone else. Second-best was not good enough.

My brother, John, was at this time going through his wild days. He had problems with his temper and had turned into a highly aggressive teenager. John was eighteen months older than I was, and in addition was large for his age. He was so powerful that while still at school he went to try out for the Welsh rugby team. He might have been selected for the squad but for an incident in which he nearly broke someone's back due to his temper. After this he was sent home, and was out of the running.

I always had a lot of respect for John, though it was respect born of fear. Often, his aggression would be directed against me. Many times he would take my clothes and return with them all torn apart, and often with blood on them. If I said anything, all hell would break loose. I was terrified of him, and used to get some serious beatings. Often I would show up at school wearing a black eye or a swollen nose.

At one point things got so bad I contemplated killing myself. I was feeling so down about my situation. Every day was a struggle, and I had to deal with constant fear—the fear of certain violence that was going to be inflicted on me.

In a movie, I had seen men stranded in the desert push themselves forward and forward until their bodies could not take any more physical stress, and they died. This was what I planned to do to end my misery. I would run and run until I killed myself.

There was a local mountain called the Folly, and on the chosen day I ran toward it, pushing myself to keep running as fast as I could. Ahead was the mountain. It looked like a long way to run, and I felt sure that to run that distance at tremendous speed would surely kill me. My heart would give up, and I would drop down dead.

I ran and ran as fast as I could, filled with anger and resentment over my whole situation.

The angrier I became, the more I wanted to kill myself. I kept going and going, and then suddenly I found myself on the top of the mountain. Since I was still alive, I turned toward the next peak, and did the same thing again. Pushing myself beyond what I thought was humanly possible, I found myself at the top of the next mountain.

I did this once more, and pushed even harder, for surely I would definitely be dead by the time I came to the top of the third mountain, but again I was still alive.

This I could not understand. Everything I had learned from the sources available to me told me that I would surely die from such a tremendous physical task, but here I was still living. I had done something that, prior to that point, I had believed was impossible. Indeed, it was impossible. But I had done it. How could this be?

Suddenly, the great depression lifted, and with it those thoughts of killing myself disappeared.

My analytical mind took over. I realized what I had just learned. The mind puts limitations on the body, yet the body is capable of so much more than the thinking mind believes. It is the mind that limits the body!

This understanding was never to leave me. Indeed, I have seen this so many times, both in others' lives and in my own. We are capable of so much more than our thinking allows. It is only the mind that creates boundaries and impossibilities.

What is so different about a world champion? Is he or she not made of the same as us—bone, blood, muscles, and so on? What is the difference? It can only be the mind.

In reality, anything is possible. If you want something badly enough, then it becomes possible. The only limit is belief. If you believe with all your heart that you can do it, then you can.

You may ask, why cannot everyone who believes in this philosophy become, for example, a world champion boxer? The answer lies in the strength of each individual's belief, and the amount of sacrifice one is willing to make. Total belief demands doing everything necessary to reach a goal.

This has to go deeper than a mere verbal belief in the mind. What I call the "feeling center" must be brought into alignment. It must become an all-embracing belief that includes total self-confidence, backed by a feeling of utter certainty in the area of the solar plexus. You have to form an emotional bond with the belief, and a total commitment to the idea, "I can, and I will."

In a state of total belief, you are without thought. You just know.

Different levels of achievement correspond to varying intensities of belief. If you do not really believe in your heart that what you are trying to achieve is worth the energy you have to put into it, this will be the obstacle that limits your level of achievement.

Just before my fifteenth birthday, school broke up for Easter. Those who decided they did not want to write any exams were allowed to leave.

That condition applied to me and to almost all the lads I went to school with. None of us was interested in academic qualifications.

I left school, and began my first job.

❈ *3* ❈

Out to Sea

MY JOB WAS working on a coal delivery truck. This appealed to me because I saw it as a way to prove how tough I was. I was like a bird that shows off its vivid colors in order to intimidate challengers. When you get behind the display, you find a frightened individual underneath.

I also saw the work as a useful complement to my boxing training. Not only could I train during sessions, I would also have a physically-demanding job that in itself was going to make me stronger.

The pay was abysmally low, even by the standards of the time. I earned five pounds and fifty pence a week. I would give my mother the five pounds, and save the fifty pence for any clothes I needed. Jack Evans, the owner of the boxing gym, had taken a liking to me, and let me train free of charge. Clothing was the only thing I needed money for.

To get to work in the mornings, I ran all the way. It must have been about four or five miles. This, too, was useful for my training.

The amount of food I ate was incredible. With all the expenditure of physical energy, I need to eat all the time. I would get so hungry I would not be fussy as to what I ate.

By now, my mother was with the man she would remain with. He was more like a father to me and my siblings than anyone else in our lives. I wonder how he and my mother ever put up with the antics my brother and I would get up to when we were teenagers. We must have been a constant source of headaches.

Although I was in training, and still preoccupied with the idea of becoming a world champion boxer, I was also dreaming of new possibilities for adventure. My imagination was fuelled by what I saw on television.

My favorite actors at that time were Bob Hope, Bing Crosby, and Humphrey Bogart. I would watch the *Road to* series, and imagine myself visiting the exotic destinations featured. When I saw the scene in the Humphrey Bogart movie where he pulls the *African Queen* through the jungle, I pictured myself doing the same thing.

In one of the Bob Hope films, the action takes place on an island filled with beautiful Hula girls. This seemed out of this world to me. The attraction was partly sex-related, as I believed that all such islands were populated by hordes of gorgeous women, but it was also related to my desire to be a hero. I was in search of adventure, and the star of the adventure was going to be me. The idea of trekking through jungles and swamps appealed to my ego.

One day, I returned from work carrying a newspaper. In it was an advertisement for jobs as merchant seamen. I said to my mother: "That's what I want to do. I'm going to be a seaman, and sail the world."

My mother replied: "You don't have the guts to do that."

I had only just turned fifteen, and my mother knew I had only made the announcement out of bravado. But because she had called me on it, my ego was put out of shape. I determined I would prove to her that I was the man I thought I was. Had my mother not challenged me, I would probably would have forgotten about the whole possibility.

I clipped the ad from the newspaper, and mailed off a letter of application, making sure my mother saw every step of the operation. From her body language, I knew she thought I was just allowing my imagination to run wild. "Come back down to earth," was her attitude.

Being young, full of pride, and with a massive ego, I had to prove a point. I told my brother and all my friends I was going to join the merchant navy. What had started as a fantasy to fuel my ego began to turn into the real thing.

Now I could not back out, even if I wanted to. But the thought of seeing all those places around the world did genuinely appeal to me.

I asked a few of the adults I knew what the merchant navy was like. One common image of merchant seamen at that time was that most of them turned gay, since they were at sea so long and had to have sex with each other because there were no women. I did not like the thought of becoming gay, but if what I was told was true, becoming gay might be inevitable. Still, the potential reward of getting to see the world for free, and being paid for it into the bargain, won me over.

My brother taunted me about the possibility of my becoming gay. He and his friend one day said that when you join the merchant navy they "give you the golden rivet." I was so naive I had to ask what this meant. The thought did scare me. I gave it some more thought, and decided my brother and his friend were just jealous and trying to discredit what I planned to do.

A few weeks later, I got a letter back saying I had been accepted. Before I knew it, I was at sea training school at Gravesend, on the southeast coast of England.

I was training as a catering boy. This was not really what I wanted to do, as I felt it was a girlie job, but since the medical exam had determined I was color blind, I was not allowed to work as a deck hand, which is what I had originally envisaged.

I got through the training without too many hitches, and secured a job with Geest banana ships. The first ship I sailed on was the *Geest Tide*, which had a run to the Caribbean.

As I began my first day on board ship, I was extremely nervous. I did not know what to do, as it was all so new to me. After a while, I learned the routine, and the rest of the trip went well.

Before we got to the islands, a few things happened that I will always remember with awe.

One day I went to empty the tea overboard, a task that was part of my daily duties. I looked out to sea and saw that the Atlantic Ocean had become as flat as a mirror. I had never seen such thing in my whole life. As far as the eye could see, the whole ocean was like one great, vast mirror. I felt as if I had entered a dream world. No one had ever told me it was possible for the sea to become so surreally flat, and I was totally unprepared for the sight.

After taking in this wondrous scene, I emptied the tea. On my way back, I turned to look back and thought I was hallucinating. Silver things were rising out of the sea and flying through the air. For some time, I pondered what they were, as I had never seen or heard of such a sight.

The next day, as usual, I went out to empty the tea. And again the sea was like a vast mirror, and lying on the deck I saw a fish with wings. This solved the mystery. What I had seen the day before was a school of flying fish—creatures I had not previously known existed.

As we neared the Caribbean islands, we were greeted by a school of dolphins swimming in front of the ship. They performed acrobatics and played games for any spectator who happened to be watching. It was like a circus show, except that it was free, and these dolphins were not in captivity, nor were they doing tricks for food. This was their natural way to be. It was a beautiful sight.

Being young and naive, I could not believe my first sight of the islanders. The people who carried the bananas to the boat wore rags and had no shoes. I had been raised in a society where it was the norm to wear shoes. Even the poorest in our society wore shoes, but seeing these people who had no shoes made me feel sad for them.

We went to the island of Dominica, and the ship had to anchor at sea while the dockworkers came out to the ship with cases and cases of bananas. They would form a chain gang and hurl boxes of bananas up from their boats to the ship.

Some of these workers were so big and muscular it made me feel like I was knee-high to a grasshopper. I was impressed by the beautiful scenery of the islands, and the simple way the islanders lived. We completed the first voyage without any problems, and sailed back to good old England.

That trip was about eight weeks all round, and I had accumulated a bundle of money by the time I got home. I treated my little sister to new clothes. Then I took all my friends out, treated them to a night of free drinking at my expense, and told tell them about my adventures. It was an ego boost, really, because I had done something they had not. I was the man of experience, or so I thought, showing off my wads of cash.

After four days at home, it was time to go back on board and to start the next trip. Part of me looked forward to this, while another part wanted to stay home with my friends in the world I knew and understood. I had been quite lonely at sea, and everything was alien to me.

Though I was still wet behind the ears, my sense of adventure got the better of me. It would have been easy to stay at home, but I would have been humiliated to begin a job, and not have what it took to complete it and succeed. Even though I was only fifteen years old, I had some self-respect, or what I thought was self-respect, so I got on board, and we sailed off again.

When we sailed passed the Azores, I asked one of the crew what the islands were that we were passing. Due to my lack of education,

31

I was clueless about geography, and when we passed them the first time, I thought we were already at the Caribbean islands!

We must have got about a day of sailing behind us, and then word came that the engine room was on fire.

I did not think too much of it at the time, because no one seemed to put too much importance to it. People reacted as if it were a minor fire that would soon be extinguished.

Then the order came to go outside on to the upper deck. By now, smoke billowed out of the engine room.

Things began to sound serious. A few people started to panic, but in general most people remained calm and in good spirits.

The ship started to lean to the port side. The engineers battled the fire in the engine room, and eventually got it under control. However, there was now no way for the ship to continue its scheduled voyage. We had to sail back to Barry dock. The ship continued to list to one side all the way back.

I WENT HOME until I got called again for my next voyage. This time I was put on another Geest ship, and again we sailed off toward the Caribbean.

We did the usual tour of the islands, and when we got to St. Lucia, a couple of West Indian ladies came on board. One knocked on my cabin door, and I let her in. I guess I was in need of company.

She got straight to the point in words that left me in no doubt as to the purpose of her visit.

"You want a f——y f——y?"

I said I would not mind.

"Five dollars," she said.

I told her I had only three dollars.

"Okay," she said.

Such was my first encounter with a lady from another country.

When we got back home, I told my friends about this incident. Many of them had by now had stints in youth detention centers.

They listened with intensity. Black girls were very rare in the valleys of Wales in those days, so this was truly a notch on the gun.

I got on for the next trip, and after some days I sat in the mess room listening to the older fellows, a bunch of Liverpudlians, talking about what they called "a dose."

This was a new term to my ears. I asked what it was, and they told me it was a sexually-transmitted disease. I vaguely remembered the concept from sex education lessons at school.

They went on to describe the symptoms of gonorrhoea, and I realized to my horror that the girl I had sex with had given me gonorrhoea.

When word got around of this, I became the laughing stock of the entire crew. It had been my first time, and trust me to catch what was available. No one had told me that venereal diseases raged out of control in those countries. I had to find out the hard way.

When we got to Barbados, I had the treatment, and thankfully got rid of it. I return to feeling my normal self again, and going to the toilet ceased to be a painful task.

On the next trip, we called in again at St. Lucia, and sure enough the same girl was there. She came to my cabin, and started her routine again.

"Hey, man, you want a f——y f——y?"

I told her that the last time we had sex, I had caught a dose off her.

She said: "No, not me, man."

Well, I knew it was her, because she was the only girl I had ever had sex with.

Suddenly, she began to rub me in my most vulnerable area. I was taken aback. I had never come across this sort of situation before.

Then she asked me again. It was a hard decision to make and, regretfully, I again said: "Yes, okay."

I just could not resist—even though I knew I stood a chance of being re-infected with gonorrhoea.

For some time afterwards, I worried I might have gotten gonor-

33

rhoea again, but the symptoms never returned. I guess it was because I had just finished the treatment for the first bout.

My sexual education was to continue. One day, I had finished my duties, and had the rest of the evening off. I decided to go to the mess room, to see if anyone was around for a chat. I went to the door of the mess room, and pulled down the handle. As the door opened, I saw two of the West Indian crew sprawled across the couch.

I looked with disbelief as I saw two men having sex with each other.

I quickly closed the door, and hurried back to my cabin in utter disbelief. For some reason, it had evoked fear in me.

After witnessing this scene, I started to have images in my mind of myself having sex with a man, and then I would feel disgusted with myself for allowing such filth to enter my mind. But the images would not go away.

After some time, I began to question my own sexuality, for these images were becoming more frequent. I had to struggle to evict them from my mind. Why were they there? I thought that what I had been told was coming true—that if you join the merchant navy, you eventually turn gay.

I became depressed by these thoughts, and by the images that would not leave me alone. It made me unhappy, and I would think and think about it. Thinking seemed to stir up the images even more strongly.

After a time, the images began to stimulate the sexual organs of my body. This caused me to think long and hard. How can I accept that I am gay? It is not right! How did this happen to me?

Then it came to me. I had been given ideas by people outside of myself. I had accepted images into my mind that were given me from the outside world. I had absorbed them without question, like someone swallowing unwanted food. They had stayed there, hidden, waiting for the right time to resurface. The West Indians on the couch had triggered my mind to create these images.

I was given the realization that it was only because I had allowed such images and beliefs to be created in my mind that I believed them. It was a choice. I had not been born with these in my mind, but had accepted them as if they were my own.

When I came to this realization, it was as though a great weight was lifted from my body, and I became at ease with myself again. I learned from this that I am whatever I believe I am. I also became aware of how the imagination exerts a powerful influence on how a person thinks, and what they believe themselves to be.

Some time after this, I saw a television documentary about a man who believed he was a woman born into a man's body. I felt sorry for this person. I realized I had won a battle as a fifteen-year-old that some people never win.

People become convinced by their own ideas. My heart goes out to them. Had this individual realized the power of the mind, he could easily have changed the outcome, and suffered so much less.

The mind can create whatever it pleases. Life can be so much better if you decide that when you get up in the morning, you will say to yourself, before you are properly awake: "Today I am going to feel good, and nothing will bother me, and I believe this with all my heart." This is something you can try for yourself.

People who pray in the morning (as long as they pray in the right way) are in effect creating their own environment for the day, much like hypnosis, but on a different level. If you believe something, then that forms the basis for your realities. You have only to believe in order to improve your life.

A hypnotist can help people give up an unhealthy habit such as smoking. When he puts his client under hypnosis, he will put images into the client's mind of how smoking cigarettes is connected to dirty things. Many people have successfully given up smoking with these kinds of image projections that are artificially put into their minds from an outside influence.

In the same way, a whole country can be seduced into believing a charismatic leader. Hitler rose to power, and committed all his evil atrocities, with the backing of millions of people. In the same way, the media can make the general public believe whatever they choose. External images and ideas are absorbed subconsciously, and become a part of your own belief system.

These images in the mind can stimulate the body, or a particular organ of the body that acts as a receptor. This can apply to, for example, the sex organ. Whatever you identify with forms a cluster you assume to be your real identity. Related thoughts coalesce and are then mistakenly conceived to be your real being.

My next trip at sea was quite an experience. The weather was not too bad when we started off, but as the trip went on, it became atrocious. The sea blew up to a gale force 12. We found ourselves in the middle of a hurricane.

As I was emptying the tea, I held on to the railings on the side of the ship, and looked up to see waves the size of houses. The chef noticed me doing this, and told me I could have been washed overboard due to my ignorance. He showed me a hatch in the main galley that could be opened to allow me to dispose of garbage while remaining safely inside.

The sea had a steady swell to it, and it seemed as everything happened in slow motion. The swell would pull the boat down slowly, then raise it back up in a continual series of eerie motions.

That was it for me. I was sea-sick all the way out, and all the way back home. It was the worst thing I have ever experienced.

After that trip, which lasted eight weeks, I concluded I was not meant for a life at sea. It was as if someone up there was saying to me: "This is not for you."

Though I only stayed with the merchant navy for nine months, in that nine months I experienced more than many people will experience over the course of several years.

I finished my last day, and returned to the valleys of Wales. I needed to find a new direction in life.

❁ 4 ❁

Back Home

HERE I WAS back home again. Secretly, I felt a failure, but I could not handle any more of that kind of life. The job was too easy, the food was too good, and though the money was good, the only thing you had to spend it on was drink. I wanted to find a life that offered more grit and excitement.

I was not surprised to learn that many merchant seamen were either alcoholic or on the verge of it—myself included, for the short time I had been a merchant seaman. Even though it was only nine months, I felt I had gotten a lifetime's worth of experience out of it. I had been through a fire at sea. I had been through a hurricane. I had caught a dose of gonorrhea, and to top it off, I was sea-sick all through the last voyage.

The sea-sickness is what wrapped it up for me. Though my sea-faring days were now at an end, this had been something I felt I needed to do.

Even if I had known beforehand how it was going to turn out, I would still have had to do it. There was a reason for it, as there is with most things in life. Certain innate qualities have to be allowed to blossom, and without the right experiences these qualities will remain hidden beneath the surface.

While I had been at sea-training school, a man had come to visit the school one day from the local army firing range. He told me that he, too, was once a merchant seaman, but had packed it in after deciding it was not for him. At this point he joined the army.

I was impressed by the stories of his adventures. Even the Northern Ireland stories struck a chord of excitement within me. At that time, any news coming out of Northern Ireland was always bad, but this did not dampen my enthusiasm.

Meeting him planted a seed in my mind as to what the next phase in my life would be.

Since I was not yet sixteen, I would not be able to join the army for another couple of years, as the minimum age for the regular army was seventeen-and-a-half. My friend told me it was better to go into the man's army, rather than to join the boy's army, for which I would then have been old enough.

In the meantime, I took a job on a building site as a laborer and tea boy. I told the foreman I was eighteen so that I would get full pay instead of a reduced youngster's wage. Since I could do the work of a man, why not?

I earned forty-five pounds a week, which in those days was a very good wage for a young lad, and compared very favorably with what my old school friends were getting.

The site I worked on was in the middle of Pontypool, where we were building a grocery store. While working there I learned to blend in with the culture of the older and more experienced construction workers.

One of the customs of this bunch was that, if we saw a young and attractive female walking past the site, we were all obliged to shout out such things as, "Drop 'em, Blossom," or "Do they go all the way up to your ass?" This created an atmosphere of macho humor.

Although some of the young ladies did take offense to this, I noticed that the majority of them laughed it off, either from embarrassment, or from the pleasure of having their ego lifted by all the male attention.

Up to this point, I had never paid a lot of notice to young ladies walking down the street in a sexually-appealing manner. But the experience of working in construction consolidated a new characteristic in my personality, and changed my thought processes to a remarkable degree. Every time a young, attractive female would walk by, I found my eyes following her, and I would fantasize about what I would like to do with her.

The fantasies this stirred up obscured my normal thinking capacity. It was at this time that the remnants of that calm and "at peace" state of mind deserted me, to be replaced by a craving for sensory stimulation. At the time, I was not fully aware of what I was losing, and what was taking its place.

A year passed, and I found myself getting closer to my seventeenth birthday. Most of the friends I went to school with were in prisons or youth detention centers. I was no angel, but just lucky not to get caught for the things I did. Perhaps I was not meant to get caught. If I had been caught, I would never have been able to get in to the army.

One day, I told my mom that I was going to join the army. My mother said: "You couldn't stick the merchant navy. What what makes you think you'll be able to stick the army?"

As before, her words only strengthened my determination to go through with this plan. The ego was working to its most concentrated degree. I was hurt, and as a result resolved even more firmly to get in to the army.

By now my old rival, John Macadam, had moved to Trevethin, and lived only a few doors away from us. We were friends and rivals at the same time, and so decided to join up together.

My first attempt at writing the army entrance exam was a failure. I made another attempt, and this time an army sergeant helpfully passed me the answers to the questions I was having trouble with. John Macadam also passed.

Whenever John was around, I always felt myself becoming more competitive. All through my secondary school days, he would give me fierce competition in track events and cross-country, but my determination to win was so strong I would never let him beat me.

As an example of our competitiveness, a few summers earlier, when we were all about thirteen, John Macadam, Clive Peploe and I decided to go and visit my brother, who was locked up in Exeter young men's prison. Due to the competitive spirit that ruled our relationship, we decided to make a challenge of it by walking almost all the way there, and all the way back.

We slept rough. Wherever we could find cover became our bed for the night. After a couple of days like this, and without any way of cleaning ourselves, we began to emit a revolting smell that followed us around. What made it worse was that that year was a particularly hot summer.

One day, we sat down near a train station to have a rest. As we did so, a train pulled up. Some women got off the train and I heard one of them gasp, and say: "I think the smell coming from those young lads is disgusting!"

When Clive Peploe took his shoes off, he nearly choked us to death with the stench. I felt sorry for him, really. He was a bit younger than John and me, and did not know what he let himself in for when he volunteered to come with us. For most of the trip we had to wait for him, as he would lag behind, and the gap between him and us got wider and wider as the journey progressed.

We got there and back okay, but for young lads of our age, this was an epic task. It was driven mostly by competitiveness.

These types of incidents showed me how energy is evoked by the power of thoughts. Our bodies were not yet fully developed, yet we achieved a task that many fully-grown adults would have had difficulty achieving.

I realized that, closely related to the way in which energy created in the mind can power the body, is the question of why we die before it is right to die.

The answer given me was that the life expectancy of the normal human being is round about seventy-five or eighty years in the western world, but this falls far short of what a human being is capable of, when one understands what is possible, and why people die before their time. This is a great psychological barrier, and one at which so many of us fall.

Many of the great teachers of the past have tried to teach mankind how to prolong life, and how to be healthy and at peace, by living in accordance with certain doctrines and principles. From their teachings come the world's religions. A common way of expressing the principle is to say that we must "die to the self". This may sound paradoxical, but in this simple teaching lies a great secret.

We have to understand the metaphorical meaning of spiritual teachings. In the beginning there was Adam, meaning Man, and Eve, meaning Woman. One of the things God told them not to do was to eat from the tree of knowledge of good and evil. But they were tempted, and so they ate from this tree. Suddenly they became aware they were naked, and covered themselves.

What are we to make of all this? For sure, it was not really a piece of fruit that one man ate, but rather the conscious development of knowledge. Man (Adam) had started to use the rational mind.

Through evolution, and the survival of the fittest, man developed a thinking mind. What, then, can we say about Man before he ate from the tree of knowledge of good and evil? What was his mind like? If there was no knowledge of good and evil, then there was no rational, thinking mind. So what remained?

When we think and formulate ideas, we are using only one part of our brain. This is the side to do with physical knowledge of the world.

But there is another side to us. This is the side connected with intuition—our artistic side, and what the mystics and yogis call samadhi. It is a state of consciousness that can be reached by stopping the mind from wandering. To be more specific, we must stop the mind from thinking and describing. This is how a person becomes one with God, or with the infinite universal soul.

Jesus went into the wilderness for forty days and forty nights to be tempted by Satan. Who is Satan? Satan is the thinking mind. And did not Buddha sit under a banyan tree to extricate himself from the worldly desires in his thinking mind? And did not Krishna teach that we should work without attachment to the results imagined by the thinking mind?

In the stock market crash of October 1929, some people were so attached to their finances they would rather take their lives than make do with fewer possessions. Their mind had allowed them to believe that they were their money, and their money was all they were.

Today it is unfortunately still the same. But is human life not worth so much more than this? Through meditation, and the correct use of the mind in everyday life, we can develop what might be called a "higher" mind.

Before one meditates, one believes the thinking mind to be what and who one is, but when one learns to meditate, one becomes detached from the thinking mind.

The birth of new awareness is like the development of a new-born baby. When awareness is developed to a certain potential, it is like having another mind that stands back quietly from all the things we do and simply watches everything. One becomes aware that all things in life are just an act, and feels as if one is playing a part in a scene. This is how it becomes, and how it feels, when one has developed to this state.

How many people waste their time trying to build an image that makes them look impressive, when in fact their lives are in tatters? They are slaves to their ideas about themselves.

There are husbands and wives who hardly see each other because they spend so much time working for career and possessions. When they do see each other, they are too tired to enjoy their time together. This causes friction; the friction causes relationship problems;

and eventually the marriage breaks up. The great universal teacher takes away all that has been worked for—gone with the bang of the judge's gavel.

This is turn creates a generation of children who do not know what it is to have a happy life. They, too, will grow up, and the cycle begins again. Who will be the one to break the cycle?

So many people complain about the way the Earth is being treated, without giving any thought as to the poor way in which they treat themselves and the people around them. Naturally, children end up copying all this. How can anyone expect harmony with the Earth, when there is no harmony in our homes?

Problems over money, power, and prestige all manifest when people develop wrong ideas about themselves. In reality, you are not the person imagined by your ideas. You are not the bank manager: that is just the job you do. You do not have a superior intellect: that is something you learned to develop.

My learning of these lessons was to continue in the army. With the recruiting sergeant's help, we passed the entrance exam and were given a date to sign up.

Unfortunately John Macadam got cold feet and never showed. I was not about to let that put me off.

I went to Cardiff and signed the forms.

After waiting for the next available training camp, I was there. I was in the army.

❊ 5 ❊

In the Army

OUR TRAINING CAMP was at a place called Cwrt-y-Gollen, not far from Pontypool. This was a good arrangement from my point of view, since I would not have far to travel whenever I wanted to visit home.

It was not long before the army discovered I was a useful boxer. Since I was a local lad, they got to hear of my reputation and were straight on to me to join their boxing team. The team needed to put on a good showing at the quarter finals of the UK championships, and I could not get out of doing my bit toward the effort. We were fighting the parachute regiment, and had to get some training in.

Our platoon sergeant was named Sergeant Evans. He used to strike the fear of God into us young recruits. He would wear his hat with the peak pulled over the top of his eyes, so that whenever he wanted to look at you, he would have to raise his chin. You would see him with his swagger stick under his arm, marching around, and shouting orders at the top of his voice in the most colorful language you could imagine.

He was certainly not for the weak-minded recruit. One of his favorite activities was testing how good his punches were by giving everyone a dig in the ribs as they stood on parade.

Soon I was well into the training, both for the boxing and for the army. One day I was training in the gym and in popped a loud-mouthed fellow who seem to know me, but I did not think I knew him. This was not unusual, since being a boxer always seemed to get you well-known.

He shouted over to me: "So you think you're a good boxer, do you? Well I'll see how good you are."

At the time I was only seventeen-and-a-half, and just a young lad. This fellow who had come into the gym to see how good I was probably close to thirty, obviously in the prime of his life, and a strong-looking man. Though not tall, he was broad and stocky, and wore rugby clothes. He looked like a typical rugby forward. He came over and got gloved up. I had the gloves put on me, too.

We began by sparring, but then he chose to turn it into a real fight.

I had all the confidence in the world in the boxing ring. Nobody could touch me, or so I believed, as I had been in the ring with some of the best in the country, and indeed in Europe. I was willing to treat it as just a spar, but this fellow needed to be put in his place. He was trying to hurt me.

This brought up thoughts of, "Why is he trying to hurt me? I have done him no wrong," and, "I don't like his attitude."

Inside me was a feeling of hurt that started at the center of my belly. The hurt then changed into a feeling of confidence, perhaps even comfort. The ring was my world. I was in control.

Now that the sparring match had turned into a fight, I decided I was going to hurt this fellow. If you will excuse my expression, I laid ten bells of shit into him.

The next day on drill parade, Sergeant Evans seemed different. He appeared apprehensive in his dealings with me. He did his usual routine before drilling us of giving all a dig in the ribs, just to make sure he imposed his authority over us.

(Many people might cry out, "Bully," and say that this sergeant should have been kicked out of the army by today's standards. But when you are going into battle, you need to be able to rely on the soldiers around you. Your life depends on them, and it is better that wimpy people be weeded out at this stage.)

This particular morning, he did his usual routine. As he came to me, I braced myself ready to receive his punch in the solar plexus.

He walked past me. This I could not understand. I was the only recruit he would never miss out. Not only that, he did this for the rest of our training period, six months altogether.

As time went by, the penny dropped. I realized the fellow who had sparred with me in the gym that day, the one I had given the hiding of his life to, just happened to be none other than good old Sergeant Evans.

Here was a man who was used to shooting his mouth off and making everybody (including me) quake in their boots. If I had known this was Sergeant Evans, I would not have been able to flatten him the way I did. He was used to people being frightened of him, and this was his source of psychological strength.

He looked so different in his rugby clothes that I had not recognized him. We were on the same level. Had I recognized him, it would have made a difference in my performance.

I took this as a useful piece of learning of how the mind colors the way we deal with situations. I had learned, too, how fear can interfere with the way you perceive what is happening and your resultant performance.

How many times have we met someone for the first time, and by the way they talk, dress, and express themselves, had an opinion as to what type of person they are? How often have we thought they evoke a sense of defensiveness, offensiveness, or something in between, and have either automatically given them our trust, or distrust, or been put off by what we think of them?

Have you seen a homeless man lying in a doorway and avoided

47

making eye contact, because they evoke in you a feeling of fear for your safety? Do you think he might rob you, given half a chance, and so you ignore him? Or perhaps he arouses compassion in you, and you search your pockets to give him money so he can buy himself a square meal. Perhaps you felt or behaved somewhere between these two extremes. His appearance caused all these varied thoughts from different passers-by.

But did you ever think he is the same as we are? Did you think he is life force, or spirit, but is just on a different learning pattern than I am, and that I am no greater than he, and he is no greater than me? For this is the truth, and all the rest is the workings of our mind.

With Sergeant Evans, this surely was the case. I had mentally granted him the superior image he took for granted, and then had unknowingly taken it away from him.

When the day for the quarter-finals came, they made a big occasion of it. Some of the top brass were there to watch the fights. They looked on us as though we were their prize animals.

The boxers were in the changing rooms readying themselves for their individual fights. The fights were arranged by order of weight, with the lightest weights up first, and the heaviest last.

As I was a lightweight, I was on third. The two before me would be the bantamweight and featherweight. Then it would be my turn.

Our trainer was a Geordie from the northeast of England. All I remember about him was his strong accent.

Finally, it was time for my fight.

I cannot count the number of times I went to the washroom that day, but I would never have allowed it to be known that I was scared shitless. The boxing competition had been the topic of conversation for some time, and a lot of people out there would be rooting for me and our team.

I got up in the ring for my fight. My knees were trembling and I began kicking my legs forward, one after the other, trying to look as though I were warming up. In reality, it was a maneuver to stop me from peeing myself! Whenever I see a boxer do this now, I still believe this is what they are doing, from my own experience of the same situation. Now I sit back and find it quite funny that almost all boxers do this with their legs before they fight.

The army had made it into a grand occasion. There was a brass band, and even the field commander of the ground forces was there. This was no small occasion.

The bell went off, and our fight began.

THE FELLOW I was fighting seemed to want to jab and move. I wanted to fight, but whenever I got close, he would jab and move away.

Again, I moved in close, and again he jabbed and backed off. I thought that if I did that too, then either there would be hardly any punches thrown, or he would make up his mind to come in and make a fight.

He did not change his tactics, and there was hardly a punch thrown. Again and again, he would jab and move away. He did not want a fight, and he was happy to keep his distance.

Once in a while, his jab would hit me on the end of my nose, which made my eyes water. I began to feel a surge of anger, as I thought: "Why won't he fight me? This is a coward's way to fight." He kept hitting and running away without allowing a fight to develop.

Had I wanted to, I could have done the same thing even better than he was doing it, and there would have been no fight at all. The anger that was aroused in my body came from the sequence of thoughts put together in my mind.

I tried everything to draw him out, but he would just not fight.

Then I spotted a weakness in his defense. As he jabbed, he would bring his left glove down below his chin, which left him open for a right hook to the chin.

As I could not catch him, I planned that every time he double-jabbed me, I would not counter. This, I hoped, would make him more confident so that he would continue to do the same thing. Sooner or later, he would do this when he was in the corner of the ring, and I would trap him and let him have it.

The bell rang for the end of the second round. Our trainer said to me: "If you don't do something, you're going to lose on points."

I could tell that the guys from my camp were losing hope of my winning. On the other hand, I was confident I was going to knock my opponent out, and I said so to my corner man.

He urged me to change my tactics, but I was feeling certain. There was no way I was not going to knock this fellow out, so strong was the rage burning in my feeling center. He was a gutless coward, who continued to hit and run. I kept my anger under control, ready to unleash it at the right moment.

The bell went for the beginning of the third round. As I had anticipated, he became more confident in his ability, and began to think I was not to be feared.

As his confidence grew, his punches became harder. What he did not know was that every punch he threw stirred up even more anger in me, and that I was holding back and allowing it to build.

He came to a corner and did his usual combination. He dropped his left glove, as I anticipated, and then I came over the top of his left jab with a ferocious right hook. Behind my right hook lay all the conserved energy and controlled anger that every one of his punches had raised in my psyche.

It was as if I had let a vicious dog out of his cage. I caught him "on the button," as they say in the boxing world, which meant on the tip of his chin.

That first punch knocked him out, but now I could not stop my surge of anger directed at him. With a flurry of punches and uppercuts, I kept him on his feet as if he were a ping-pong ball bounced in the air with a table-tennis racket.

Finally, the referee managed to drag me off him. As he pulled me back, my opponent fell on his front as if he were a tree that had just been hacked down.

He hit the floor with no sign of life.

I had knocked him out cold.

The roof went up in the air as all the lads in the training camp with me screamed and cheered. I was caught up in the glory they projected on to me. It was a feeling I had only ever known at times like these.

I noticed there was a bit of concern among the officials as they called for the doctor. The young man was still motionless. No sooner had I reached the high of victory, than I was brought down to earth by the thought I might have killed him. If only I had let him fall to the floor with the first punch. But I had kept at him.

As the minutes passed by, there was still no sign of movement. What had been a mad blast of applause and cheering only minutes before was now transformed into silence. Except for occasional whispers, you could have heard a pin drop as we waited for the doctor.

My heart sank. I could remember that feeling of dread from only one other time, when my best friend Pete Murphy and I once stumbled upon a dog that was dead. Its body was slung on a disused rubbish tip.

Nearby we found some old railings. One of the uprights was shaped like a spear. Out of curiosity we decided to spear the dead dog. First Pete did it, and then I had a go. Afterwards, I had this feeling of remorse for what I had done. Even though the dog was dead, I felt a sickness in my stomach I will never forget.

There I was praying that this young lad lying on the canvas would be okay. That was all that was important to me at that moment. The glory of victory had left me.

The doctor climbed into the ring and examined the young fellow. Then a stretcher was brought to the ring, and the medics carried him off. Still I saw no sign of life in him. I asked if he was okay, and to my great relief, they told me he was.

Although the image of being a boxer was a good way to earn respect, in my heart I did not have it in me to want to seriously hurt anyone. These experiences taught me that. But the need to be somebody, and the need for respect in society, were stronger.

It was not long before I put this incident to the back of my mind, for news of the fight spread to a battalion that was on duty in Belize at the time. Even the field commander was so impressed by this fight that he came personally to offer me his congratulations on such a splendid fight.

The strength of the ego was stronger than any feelings of compassion in my mind at that time. Like any other seventeen-and-a-half year old lad, I rode it for what I could get.

I finally finished my training, completing the whole six months, including battle camp. On my eighteenth birthday I found myself in an airplane flying to Belize.

"WHAT A BIRTHDAY present," I thought to myself. I was looking out of the airplane window, and the thought occurred that I could not possibly forget this birthday. The plane went to first to Gander airport in Canada. From there we flew on to Belize, finally reaching the base camp.

On our arrival, a sergeant showed up wearing a tank top and shorts. He immediately asked which of us was the boxer. I did not want to say anything, as I had decided I wanted some new adventures. I knew that boxing would put a stop to that.

Not only that, but I was nervous of getting straight into boxing. I was in a foreign country and unsure of myself. I did not yet know what was on offer. I was willing to stay in the background for the time being.

Since none of us admitted to being "the boxer," the sergeant asked again. He went on to say that he knew one of us was a boxer, so who was it? Still I did not own up. Then he gave us an earful of verbal abuse and stomped off.

The next day he turned up again, and asked yet again, and with the same verbal abuse left again.

It started to become a bad situation, so in the end I had to own up. The next thing I knew, I was in training with the boxing squad. They were getting ready to fight the team from the Belize police force.

Their trainer and our trainer both appeared on a local radio station, and I will always remember what the Belize police trainer said, "If any of your lads are listening, don't show up tomorrow, because we are going to give you the thrashing of your lives."

I could feel surges of adrenaline go through my body, and again, as I had so many times in the past, I experienced the need to repeatedly go to the washroom to relieve myself.

The next day, at the weigh-in, we had a chance to eye up our prospective opponents. They were all black, full of confidence, doing the alley shuffle, and swaggering around to intimidate us. They made a good job of it.

Our lads sat down looking nervous. These Belize police officers were gifted with exceptional physiques. They all had bodies shaped like inverted pyramids. Our lads had only normal, everyday physiques, and were nothing special to look at. Had you met them on the street, you would not have known they were boxers.

The day of the fights came, and we traveled to a place called Bird's Isle. We walked across a causeway that took us on to the island.

I had never seen anything like this before. It was a little island specially arranged for the purpose of boxing. The ring was in the middle, and the spectators' seats surrounded the ring and rose above it.

I could not begin to count the number of people who were there. All of them were rooting for the Belize police team.

The first fight started, and our lad stopped his opponent. In the second fight, the same thing happened. Then the third fight, which was mine. I also won.

As the day went by, it became obvious that these lads were not well-trained boxers, and we gave them a thrashing. It came to a point that some of their lads would have to be manhandled into the ring to fight, only to receive the inevitable beating.

Before the fight, I was shaking in my shoes from the thoughts my mind gave me. At one point, on the walk over to the island, I felt like I wanted to run away from all this, but I knew I had to face it. My pride would never allow such a cowardly act as running away.

I should have known better. One of mankind's greatest problems is that he forgets, just as I did. I had forgotten the lessons that I had learned: that the mind makes limitations that cut short what you can really do. This I knew! How many more times would it take before I learned it permanently?

After the fights, we had time off from boxing training, and were allowed into our own companies and sections. Finally, I had a chance to do all those things I had imagined I would do when I was younger. Now I could go into the jungle like Humphrey Bogart, or like the heroes of the other films that had inspired me to think how great the army would be.

We were getting ready to go on exercise into the Belize jungle. Though Belize is now independent, at that time it was a self-governing British colony, and the British maintained a military presence there. Neighboring Guatemala posed a threat, and it was in British interests to keep ground forces in Belize.

My dreams of adventure as a young boy began to come real when we all had to bivvy up and blend into the scenery of the jungle. I was already an expert at this. During the exercise I lived in luxury compared to everyone else, since I made a covering out of all the materials the jungle offered. I was good at knowing how to cut wood quickly in the short amount of time available to us to bivvy up.

Most of my colleagues, including the platoon sergeant and the officer in charge, slept out in the open. I had always thought how great it would be, to be doing what I was doing now. The reality was that the conditions were unbearable. Although I know the human body has the ability to adapt, the truth was it was uncomfortably hot, there were mosquitoes everywhere, and the insects would keep you awake at night. This left you tired and irritable during the day. The insects would make tracks over you. After a while you became so tired, you would not even bother to knock them off when you were trying to put your head down for the night.

You would also be semi-dehydrated. The only water you had was what you could carry in your water cans, and you were issued only two of these.

On one occasion, when we were dehydrated, the platoon commander decided to send out a reconnaissance party to look for water. We had been sweating, and could not possibly replace needed water with the small amounts we carried in our water bottles.

The recce party returned with a reported sighting of water, and the company commander gave orders for everyone to hand in their water bottles.

Given that we were on a combat exercise, I had a strong sense these fellows were going to get caught. If they were, we would be stuck in the middle of the jungle with no drinking water.

The other soldiers emptied their bottles into their stomachs, and gave both bottles to the recce team. I gave just one empty bottle, so sure was I they were going to get caught. The full one I kept and resisted the strong temptation to drink all of it in one go.

The recce party went off, leaving everybody except me with no water. As time went by, they became overdue, and then the news came back they had been captured.

We were zapped. If this had been real battle conditions, we would have perished.

The interesting thing was, when the news came back, I was not at all surprised. This was not because I was an experienced soldier. I just had a gut feeling this was what was going to happen. It was such a strong compulsion that I overcame the temptation to go along with the order to hand in both water bottles along with everyone else.

How did I know? I have heard stories of soldiers in Vietnam who would come to a place where they were supposed to go down one track, but would choose the other track, theoretically going in the wrong direction, but by so doing avoided ambushes laid down for them by the Vietnamese. Perhaps this was a similar incident.

Finally, the tour came to an end, and we were on our way back to the UK.

WE ARRIVED IN the Royal Welsh Fusiliers' barracks in Tidworth, in the south of England. It was time for me to find out what life was like in home base.

Life there turned out to be like a regular nine-to-five job, except that I would have to carry out the occasional stint of guard duty. That meant I might have to stay at the barracks for the weekend, or else do a night shift during the week.

These duties lasted only for a short period, since I was still a part of the battalion boxing team. Because we were getting ready for championship fights, we were excused most normal duties. It also meant we were in training almost all the time, and even had our own special tracksuits imported from the United States.

We were treated like royalty. The army arranged for us to have a special diet, and compared with the rest of the squaddies, we were really spoiled.

The evenings were spent either going to the local town, where they had a bowling alley, or to the local disco, Mooltan's, which was open two nights a week. Other locations for nights out included the nearby towns of Salisbury and Andover. It was better to go to Salisbury or Andover on Friday nights, as you did not have to worry about getting back to barracks in time for reveille in the mornings.

I remember one such night. We had not long come back from Northern Ireland, and I and two friends from the boxing team decided to go to Salisbury.

Going out with guys from the boxing team turned out to be a

serious mistake. In the army, your colleagues become like family. After a while there is a close bonding.

We had a good drinking session, and did the usual things for off-duty soldiers. We went to a disco, got drunk, and had a punch-up. The night seemed to go by quickly.

When the disco finished, we decided to make our way back to barracks. We could not get a taxi, as they were all busy, so we decided to walk from Salisbury to Tidworth, about a fifteen-mile walk.

By now we were all quite drunk. I was not used to drinking at that time. Because we were training three to four times a day, we were super-fit, and any alcohol in the system would have a much more concentrated effect than it would have had if we had not been in training.

As we headed along the road, Bobby Kinsey noticed some cars parked in a parking lot. He decided to try the doors of one of the cars. I suspect he would not have had this idea had it not been for the beer.

Suddenly, and I do not know where from, a policeman appeared and asked Bobby: "Is this your vehicle?"

Bobby said yes.

The policeman asked Bobby his name, got out his walkie-talkie, and started to make a call asking for confirmation of the ownership of the vehicle.

When Bobby realized what was happening, he knocked the walkie-talkie out of the policeman's hand, and with his other hand punched the policeman in the face.

It happened so quickly, I could not believe what I had just seen. I thought I had left these kinds of things behind me in Wales. I did not expect to see this, and stood gazing in disbelief.

Then I realized the shit we had just gotten into. Suddenly we split. We each ran in a different direction. I decided that running on the road would be a bad choice, as the police would be able to catch up in no time.

My first instinct, then, was to get the hell off the roads. Nearby was a high wall and I clambered over it. As I did so, I saw what I believed were Chinese gravestones, though to this day I do not know for sure what they were. I only know they looked Chinese.

There were a lot of overgrown bushes, and I appeared to be at the back of someone's property, where there were plenty of trees. I thought it would be a good place to hide until I could think of something better.

I lay down. The alcohol and the run had taken their effects, and I fell into a heavy sleep.

The next thing I remember is waking up. I did not know where the hell I was, and I could not remember how I got there. I did not remember anything about the policeman, nor did I have any inkling of the trouble that was looming on the horizon.

I climbed over the wall and started on my way back to the camp. I got up to the Salisbury roundabout when I saw a police car.

In a flash it all came back to me. The police car came toward me and screeched to a halt. I started to run like shit, but then another police car appeared and screeched to a halt, and then another.

Panic grabbed me. By now, the police had all stopped their vehicles, and were giving chase on foot.

I ran one way, and saw a policeman coming at me. I stopped, pulled at him, then ducked to the side. His momentum caused him to fly through the air, and he landed flat on the ground.

When I changed my direction, I was met by another policeman. I do not know what happened there, but he also ended up on the ground. Then another.

Because I kept running, they did not have a chance to gather around me. My instinct was to defend myself. I had to escape.

The whole of Salisbury police force must have been out that night. They were out for blood, as one of their own had been assaulted.

I found that, because I kept running and changing direction, I was able to keep them spread out, and they were unable to form a group around me. I only had to deal with one at a time. They were a very unfit bunch, and I could run rings around them.

I was doing fine. I had made myself a clearing after yet another policeman had gone over, and it should have been plain sailing, as I could see the way out of it. I was aiming for the fields, since they would not be able to catch me once I got to open country.

I put one foot in front of the other and my foot hit something. It must have been a broken paving slab. I fell over, and in seconds the police were on top of me and had overpowered me.

They pulled my arms behind my back and slapped a set of hand-cuffs on my wrists. They put the handcuffs on as tight as humanly possible, so that the slightest movement on my part resulted in incredible pain. Then they handcuffed my ankles together, also as tightly as possible. I was carried like a skewed pig to the police car and driven to Salisbury police station.

The police dragged me up the concrete steps, dropped me at the top, and then dragged me inside. They were not at all happy with me, not by a long shot.

Bobby and Clacker had already been caught, and were seated in one of the rooms in the police station. The police took the handcuffs off my ankles, but left the ones on my wrists. By now the pain was becoming excruciating, but something inside me would not allow me to give them the satisfaction of knowing I was in agony.

They decided to put us into a cell. Without trying to look desperate, I asked one of them: "Are you going to take these handcuffs off now?" He went back to get the keys and removed the handcuffs. It would take nearly a year for my wrists to return to normal.

As I sat in the cell looking at what a miserable sight it was, I thought to myself: *I would not like to be in one of these places for too long.*

THE ALCOHOL WAS still affecting the way I was thinking, and I started doing something to kill time. At that time, the great Bruce Lee had just made his most famous film, *Enter the Dragon*. It had infused a lot of super-human fighting energy into younger people's impressionable psyches.

I was one such young person. Unbeknownst to anyone else, I was in fact none other than Bruce Lee. We had photos of him all over our barrack room walls. Being the boxing team, we were drawn to such role models.

Wanting to be as much like Bruce Lee as possible, I had acquired a pair of nunchukas, and would practice regularly. This was one of the most excruciating periods in my life. In the hands of an untrained user, nunchukas can often hit one in the most painful of places. Once I keeled over from one blow I gave myself in the groin. This put me off for quite some time, and the next time I practiced, I was much more cautious.

My imagination began to wander as I sat in the cell. I remembered how impressed I was with an exercise Bruce Lee would do. He could do push-ups balancing himself only on his thumbs.

This was a challenge I had already taken on, and I had achieved a certain amount of expertise in the art of these thumb push-ups. Many a time I would impress my boxing colleges with them. I began to do the push-ups off my thumbs in the cell.

As I was doing them, one of the police officers came to check up on me by looking through the peephole in the door. I did not think any thing of it.

I heard him walk away, and then shortly afterwards I heard some more footsteps come up to the cell door. This time it was a whole group of them, and a discussion took place along the lines of how they intended to teach me a lesson for assaulting their colleagues.

Expecting the door to open at any moment, I got ready to defend myself. I was not at all frightened. I was in fighting mode, and the effect of the beer had not yet worn off.

Another voice said: "Have you seen him, and what he did tonight?" Then he continued: "I'm not going in there."

After this, I heard them walk away. This made my ego bigger than ever. They could not have begun to realize the effect their respect had on this young, impressionable lad. Was my ego ever going to come back down to earth after this?

Unfortunately, or perhaps fortunately, my ego was soon cut back to size. The haze of my thinking cleared, and reality dawned upon me. I could well get kicked out of the army for this.

I was dreading it. The regimental police came down and picked us up, and took us back to the camp in Tidworth. We were under arrest for a couple of nights. Then we were allowed back to our barrack rooms, but we were put on "jankers" and given all sorts of extra duties until the day we were due in court.

I was sure I was going to get kicked out of the army, for I had seen that happen to other people for much lesser crimes. As it turned out, I was charged with actual bodily harm and grievous bodily harm to police officers. One had a broken arm, another had a broken leg, and others had minor bruises. I was really worried.

Something that had begun as an innocent night out had turned into this simply because Bobby had decided to hit the police officer. I made it even worse for myself because of what happened at the roundabout. If only I had stayed in that night, none of this would have happened. But you cannot go back. It is easy to be perfect in hindsight, but what was done was done.

Now we had to await our comeuppance.

The time dragged by, and the army eventually decided they were going to defend us in civilian court and sent along an officer to defend us. He came up with a story that we had just come back from Northern Ireland and that we were just letting our hair down, so to speak. We were expecting to go down, as assaulting a police officer was a serious charge.

I did not have just one charge against me, but a whole list of them, so I thought I was especially certain to go down.

The court case came to an end, and thankfully we were practically let off with only suspended prison sentences. Mind you, the army made sure we paid for it. My pay was stopped for a period, and I had no money for months afterwards, and we were also given extra duties.

I was surprised to learn I was still in the army. But it all made sense. We were the pride and joy of our commanding officer. We were his special little boxers, and he was not going to let us go so easily. As long as the army sees that you are willing to take what they give you, it will go to your credit, especially as this kind of incident showed we had the "attitude" the army saw as being a valuable asset.

After the dust had settled, we were hard into the boxing. There was nothing else we could do. No money. Nothing. We had food and shelter, and that was it.

Apart from the use of the gym, I would go to the Mooltan (the local disco), but had no money to spend. We had, though, just finished the championship fights, where we won the title of UK Champions, so we were treated like royalty.

I started to get paid again. It seemed like a lifetime of not having money. It can get you down at first, before you adjust to living like a monk.

One night, I went out to the Mooltan, and saw one of the boxers who was in my team having a argument with, and threatening, a young woman who had a pint of beer in her hand. I knew he would not think twice about decking her, so I went over and asked her: "Do you need any help?"

She told me quite plainly to f—— off, so I walked off and left her to it.

Nothing came of it. I think the other boxer picked up on the fact he was being watched.

After she finished making a scene with him, she came over and asked me if I wanted a pint of beer. I said: "No, thanks. I don't drink."

At the time this was true, because I had decided booze and I did not get along too well. Not only that, it would interfere with my training. I had found that after you get to a certain point in your fitness, a single pint of beer could set you back about two weeks' training. You become so highly tuned that you are sensitive to subtle disturbances in your body.

I never thought any more of the whole thing. Then, one night, Bobby Kinsey asked me if I wanted to go out, and I said yes.

We went to a little pub in Tidworth that all the squaddies would use, and there in the pub I saw the very same lady who had been in the incident the week before. Bobby wanted to sit and chat them up. I was interested in the Canadian lady who was with her, so I sat with them.

They went to the ladies', came back, and swapped places. I took this as a sign that the Canadian lady did not take to me. Later I found out they had traded places on the initiative of the Canadian lady's friend, who was named Jayne.

I was not all that impressed by Jayne. She was not my type. I liked women who were feminine, and did not drink their beer from pint glasses. Though it is much more common now, this was the first time I had ever seen it, and I thought that only men drank from pint glasses. In fact, I was not even used to seeing women in bars, because that was frowned upon in Wales.

Bobby decided he wanted to have the Canadian girl. He kept sticking pints of beer under my nose and eventually my resistance to not drinking broke down. I started to drink in rounds.

He asked me to stick with this Jayne. I was getting more drunk by the minute and I said: "No way. I'm not attracted to her."

Bobby kept pestering me throughout the evening. As the night went by, Jayne seemed not to look so bad, and in any case I could not let my friend down. He had fallen madly in love with the Canadian girl, or should I say with the idea of having her. We went back to her place and did the business with them.

When I woke up in the morning, I realized that once again I found myself in a predicament I had not wished to be in. And, again, the same two factors were involved: drink, and Bobby Kinsey.

I managed to get out of the house on the pretense that I would come and see her that same night after we finished training. In truth, I had no such intention.

A short time later, Jayne told me she was pregnant.

I decided I would have to leave the army to be with her—without waiting to get permission.

I went absent without leave, and became a man on the run.

❋ 6 ❋

Absent without Leave

S HORTLY AFTER I went AWOL, and so sacrificed my army career, I discovered Jayne was in fact not pregnant.

This was not good news. I had been ambitious in the army, and wanted to join the Special Air Service (SAS) regiment. It was no small decision to go absent, and it was only Jayne's supposed pregnancy that had motivated my decision. Now she told me she was not pregnant.

Then, by a strange twist of events, she did become pregnant.

We moved into an apartment in Dudley, in the West Midlands of England. Our first impression was that it was a shabby little place. Fortunately, we had the money to turn it from what had been a dreary apartment into a cozy place to live.

However, the money was not going to last forever. Sooner or later it was going to run out.

I found four weeks' work as a bricklayer's laborer in Bilston. I grabbed at this opportunity, as it was at least a start. When I started the job, it dawned on me how this was a complete turnaround from what I had been used to in the army.

For the last three years, I had been used to having a life of leisure, training all day, eating good food, and enjoying plenty of time to myself. Suddenly, I was now on a job that required twelve hours of my time a day, seven days a week, with only fifteen minutes break in the morning and a half-hour break in the afternoon.

Still, my determination to earn money was strong, since if I did not, there was nothing else to fall back on, as I was an absentee from the army. I worked under a false name and so was assessed at an emergency tax rate, but even so the money was still good.

This was the hot summer of 1976. Being outside during a heat wave, we were all parched most of the time, and needed to be constantly drinking some form of refreshment.

It was a common practice that, when we needed relieve ourselves, we would get in the lift, go down to the ground, walk some distance to the urinals, and then come back to the job. On one particular day during the heat wave I was bursting to go but was very busy, so I could not afford to take that much time away from the job.

I grabbed an empty pop bottle, went into the lift to provide cover, and relieved myself in the bottle. Then I put the bottle down and rushed back to the job, forgetting completely about having left it there.

A couple of hours later, we were less busy and decided to go down to the works cabin for our tea break. We all got in the lift, and as I was chatting to one of the bricklayers, I noticed out of the corner of my eye one of the men bending down to pick something up. I turned around, and as I did so, saw him pick up the bottle I had urinated into. He unscrewed the top and brought the bottle to his lips.

My mouth opened to say something, but it was too late. The damage had been done, and I would not have won any brownie points had I told him at this rather late stage. Not only that, but my job depended on getting on well with these brickies. If they did not like me, I could be out of a job in no time.

He took a big gulp and swallowed. My mouth wide open, I

looked into his eyes waiting for the reaction of disgust.

There was none. I was amazed. He then passed the bottle on to one of the other bricklayers, and to my amazement the same series of actions took place. The second bricklayer then passed it on to the next, until five of them had a drink from it.

I was offered the bottle, too, but as the liquid was a bright orange color due to my dehydration, I politely turned it down. Given the lack of reaction, I began to think that someone had put another bottle down, and the one I had urinated into had disappeared.

As the last bricklayer took a swig, everyone was watching. He took the bottle from his mouth and spat out the liquid in disgust. As he did so, there were roars of laughter from all the brickies who had drunk some before him. I was then certain this was indeed the same bottle I had urinated into. I kept the guilty secret to myself, though!

These men were a breed unto themselves. Not only would they work twelve-hour shifts, seven days a week, they would then go out clubbing in the evenings.

One of the men, Frank, had the same routine every night. After the pubs closed, he would always end up in the same Indian restaurant with all the other bricklayers. He would order the same food, eat half of it, and at 2:30 A.M. would collapse head-first on to his plate, his beard saturated by his vindaloo curry, and fall fast asleep.

The most admirable thing was that he, and the rest of the brickies, would never fail to be on the job on time at 7:30 A.M., raring to go. As a young lad, I had a lot of respect for them.

It did not take them long to suss out I was AWOL from the army, but they were really good to me. They appreciated that I was a good laborer. By now, the four hundred laborers who had been on the job when I first started had dwindled down to just two of us, plus the six bricklayers. This was six months down the line, so I had gotten more work than I had thought from what was supposed to be a job that would last only four weeks.

By this time the project was all but complete, and I was offered a job with the construction firm. I did not take it, as it would have meant uprooting ourselves again to go to somewhere near Newcastle, and by this time I was totally exhausted and needed a break. We parted company.

By now, Jayne and my relationship had taken a turn for the worse. Arguments would start, and I was not capable of handling them. I would just walk out the door and leave her to it.

In those days, I was not used to arguing. I just could not see any point in two people shouting verbal abuse at each other. To me, it was a totally alien thing to do.

As time went on, Jayne would stop me from leaving through the front door by standing in my way. One day, after a lot of these sessions of abuse, I physically moved her out the way.

Then she struck me.

This straightaway made me feel extremely emotionally upset. I had done no wrong, and I could not understand her hitting me. There was great surge of what I can only call negative emotion. She had hurt me, and as far as I was concerned, I did not deserve it.

The next time I moved her out of the way more forcefully, and then made sure I did not come back home for some time. I felt the pangs of anger, since I could not understand why someone could get like this for such trivial things, and then hurt me physically. This in turn made me feel: "How would she like it, if I hit her?"

As time went by, these thought-patterns were becoming a regular thing for my mind to concoct. They were slowly growing into something real.

I was aware of this. Though I did not like it, I was not advanced enough in years and wisdom to overcome it and hold myself in check.

In time, the forceful movement turned into pushing her out of the way. The push turned into a slap. She was a very strong personality. I could see in her the result of a child becoming an adult without ever experiencing any form of correction. There was no self-control.

I was watching a child who stomped her feet and always got her way. I had to take on the work that her father had not done, for whatever reason, otherwise my life could turn into a living hell, always having to give in to the whims of such a person.

Only the fact that she was pregnant, and that I was on the run from the army, kept us together.

Shortly after my twenty-first birthday, my first son was born. This was the best birthday present I could ever have had. Here was my very own son, and I thought the world of him.

On occasion, we would go down to visit Jayne's father, who lived in Gosport, on the south coast of England. Jayne's father had broken up with her mother and married another woman, Bette, who already had a daughter two years older than Jayne.

One day, Jayne decided to go and visit Bette's daughter. I had never met her before, and Jayne wanted to introduce us.

Her name was Kaye.

WE WENT TO Kaye's place and rang the doorbell. Kaye came to the door and let us in. She invited us to sit down, and offered us a cup of tea.

Kaye had short, blonde hair and vivid blue eyes, was smartly dressed, and had a lovely figure. Her house was spotless, bright in decor and color, with flowers everywhere. She had a young daughter who looked like a little angel with her long blonde hair and big blue eyes.

As I sat down taking in the scenery, I looked at Kaye, and the strangest thing happened to me. She seemed to be surrounded by a mist. I rubbed my eyes, but this made no difference. I felt a very strong attraction toward her, and had to reason with myself that this could never be. I was with someone else, and I had a family to look after, but still I felt as if I knew Kaye. I did not know how this could be, as this was the very first time I had ever met her—or so I thought at the time.

CHAPTER 6

For a long time after this, I thought about Kaye often. The best part of it was that not many words passed between us, yet she was so strongly imprinted on my mind that, quite often, I would catch myself daydreaming about her.

I met her another three times after that. As the years went by, things changed, but I never forgot how she evoked in me this feeling that she was someone who was close to me, and a very special kind of person.

By now, I had a job with a chemical firm called Robinson Brothers in West Bromwich. To overcome the problem of having no National Insurance number to match my false name, I was using my brother's insurance so that the army could not track me down. It took a lot of getting used to when someone would address me as "John." Many times I would hear them call "my" name, and would fail to reply. I automatically thought they were calling someone else.

While I was there, aiming to keep my head low because I was on the run, an incident occurred that had never happened in all the hundred and fifty years that Robinson Brothers had been in business.

We had regular meetings of our branch of the labor union. I noticed how the union chief would say his thing, then call for a vote. The majority always voted for whatever he suggested, even if it meant taking money out of their own pockets. He would phrase his proposal in such a way that it would convince them it was in their own best interests to agree to it.

The union chief was better looked after by the management than anyone else in the works. When I had put these thoughts together, and realized how these people were being led, I conceived the idea that if this could be done so easily, I would see if I could get a pay raise using my newfound knowledge of the human psyche.

I decided to test my theory by spreading rumors. The first thing I did was to tell the night shift that all the lads on the day shift were dissatisfied with their wages, and were most certainly voting to go out on strike at the next union meeting. Then I spread the same rumor that the other shifts were most certainly going out on strike. I would finish by asking if they were going to back us.

The reply was: "Yes, if all your shift are going out, we'll have to, too." This rumor then spread throughout the factory to all the shifts. By the time the next union meeting took place, I stood up and spoke my piece.

The next thing, we were all out on strike for higher pay.

There were some who did not want to go on strike, but the majority voted in favor. One of the lads phoned up the local news papers, and they made a front-page story of a chemical factory that had never had trouble of this sort in its hundred and fifty years of existence, with a photograph of myself and some of the others standing in a picket line.

Of all the things for me to do! I was taking a risk, as I was on the run from the army, and here I was on the front of the local paper for everyone to see. Luckily, there were no comebacks. In the end, management decided to give us our pay raise.

This consolidated my knowledge of how people can be impregnated with thoughts from outside influences, and be totally unaware how these things can control them. People can be almost hypnotized into doing something. It only needs one thought from one person to do this.

This is the same way newspapers mold the opinion of the general public, not because it is their opinion, but because their minds have been saturated with the ideas of the person who wrote the article.

I find this a very dangerous trait in the human population. Everyone should ask themselves about their own political views. Are they really your own ideas, or are they ideas picked up via mass hypnotic suggestion, playing on your greed?

It is said that the Millennium Dome in London was brought to its knees by such a phenomenon. The papers gave it bad publicity from which it never recovered. But if you ask anyone who has

71

actually been there, they will tell you it was a great and enjoyable experience. Yet from the start of the project, it was always said it would lose money.

This is often the case in any new venture, as many business people know. But the papers magnified this and drove into the public mind and imagination that it was going to be a flop, and brought this about by the use of mass hypnosis.

One night while I was working at Robinson Brothers I had a dream. In the dream I saw what I took to be the end of the world. I was at work, and everybody was running in all directions. They were all being engulfed by a red haze. It was so terrifying that I woke up in a cold sweat, shaking from top to bottom. The impression was so terrifying it took me several hours to calm down and get over it.

A few weeks passed, and I woke up one morning, turned on the news, and heard that there had been an accident at Robinson Brothers.

One of the process pots at the chemical plant had blown up. Nobody had died, but a few had been taken into hospital for treatment. The works were closed down while they repaired the damage.

I returned to work when the plant was up and running again. There were all sorts of rumors circulating about the incident. I did not take too much notice until I heard, from the horse's mouth so to speak, one of the men who had actually been there and experienced the explosion, explaining what had happened.

He described seeing a red haze that had engulfed everyone who was there. He said he saw people running in all directions and had thought it was the end of the world. When he said this, I realized he was describing the scene I had seen in my dream some weeks earlier.

How could that be? How could I have seen this happen three weeks before it had taken place?

I have questioned this many times. Even to this day, I sometimes experience seeing things in dreams before they happen. I am sure there are many more people out there beside myself who have similar experiences.

I have also become aware that these dreams occur more frequently when I practice meditation on a regular basis. I have pondered this phenomenon many times, and what it means exactly to me.

I believe there is a part of the human being that is independent of the flesh, bone, and blood, and that has the ability to travel while the physical part of the body is at rest, or asleep. You can call this phenomenon whatever you please—the soul, the astral body, or whatever.

Not only has the soul the ability to leave the physical body, it can also travel in time. Since it can travel forward, I would surmise that it can also travel backward. As yet I have had no conclusive proof from my own experience that this is so, but I am told from the experience of others that this is indeed the case.

Taking this into consideration, what can we say about time, or should I say, what we call "time."

Time is measured by days, with twenty-four hours representing one rotation of the Earth. This rotation is broken down into twenty-four units, or hours, which are in turn broken down into smaller units of sixty minutes. Minutes are further subdivided into seconds, and so forth.

So in reality, time measurement is a measurement of the motion of the Earth. What we call the future is in effect the number of times the Earth will turn on its axis.

What can be concluded from these facts are, first, that what man calls time—the future, and the past—are in fact concoctions of the mind helpful for measuring certain aspects of daily life; and second, if man has the ability to go forward in time, then we must conceive of time itself in a new way.

The best approach that fits all the evidence is that the phenomenon of time does not exist outside of the mind. Time is only in existence because of a utilitarian need of mankind.

Our true situation is that we live in the "is" phenomenon, in the middle of what we call the present, but also able to look at what we call the past and the future.

It is like a geneticist who, when looking into a gene, can see what potential directions for growth that gene will generate. Future potentials are already written into the gene.

Consider also the fact that so many people who are termed psychics, clairvoyants, mediums, and the like, can already see what we call the future. This future is simply the "is". It is already there, and there is only a limited number of options, which are all innate, and any of which is ready to develop under the right conditions.

In place of time, I suggest we use the concept of growth. Growth on a molecular level corresponds to physical movement, as for example in the case of the Earth's movement, which we mistakenly call time. It is all about motion, and growth is motion, and this motion is what man perceives as time.

Take another example. Many mystics have used a glass ball or tarot cards to see into the so-called future, and have done so quite accurately. But just what are they doing? Are they really seeing the future as if on a television screen?

I suggest not. They use these things to stimulate that part of their sensory apparatus that can perceive such things, for it is always there, and it is just a matter of being able to exercise the sensory apparatus needed to perceive this "is".

From human genes the scientist can, with the right apparatus and knowledge, predict the characteristics of the fully-grown individual. So too can the clairvoyant or mystic use his sensory apparatus to see the "is".

TWO YEARS PASSED and Jayne was pregnant again.

The pressure in the relationship was becoming unbearable. It reached a stage where she put a knife in my back.

Luckily I was able to avoid the full length of the knife entering my body, because I moved at just the right time. A second longer, and things could have been much worse for me.

That killed it for me, and I decided I was going to hand myself back over to the army. I was more willing to face what they had to give out to me rather than take any more of the treatment Jayne was dishing out.

As there was another child on the way, this was a difficult decision, but I had tried everything in my power to resolve the situation. Despite my best efforts, our relationship was becoming more and more violent. It would just get worse, and it would not be good for the children to see what would have become of us staying together.

It was not good for them, and moreover it was not what I wanted for the rest of my life. It was time to do something.

I decided to turn myself in.

❊ 7 ❊

Giving Up

I WENT TO the local police station and handed myself in. They
took me to Lichfield barracks, and then to Cwrt-y-Gollen army
camp near Abergavenny.

It had been five years since I was last at Cwrt-y-Gollen. I had
come full circle, with a broken relationship, one child, and one more
on the way—who, due to my own actions, I thought I would never
see again. I had made a right mess.

Since I had voluntarily turned myself in, the army placed me
on open arrest, and I was not locked up all day as I had thought I
would be. This gave me a certain amount of freedom. I was beginning to think I had done the right thing, until who should appear
at Cwrt-y-Gollen but Jayne.

Jayne was sorry for what she had done. I could see she was
taking it badly. She was pregnant, in tears, and I could not turn
her away.

We decided we would get a place back in my hometown and
start afresh. Perhaps things would be different without the pressure
of my continually being in hiding.

The army gave me a choice. I could remain with the army if I first did a stint in Colchester ("the Glass House"), or I could take a discharge.

I decide to take the discharge. I could not see how it would serve any useful purpose for me soldiering on in the army with a family. I had seen other squaddies have problems being married with that kind of lifestyle. It was a road that inevitably led to trouble. Had I felt more comfortable in the relationship, I would have surely soldiered on. But though I liked the army, I concluded it was not meant to be.

We put in for public housing. Because I had just come out of the army, I went straight to the top of the housing list, and in no time we were in subsidized housing back in Trevethin, close to my mother. I had come back to my roots.

I got a job with a local coal delivery firm, and soon picked up all my old contacts in the boxing world and started to train again. How I had missed the smell of sweat and leather, and the high after each training session was over. I was back doing what I liked to do most.

Jayne went into hospital to have the baby by cesarean section. I waited outside the hospital in the parking lot in an old Bedford camper van I had bought. I wanted to make sure I would be there for the birth of our child.

Everything went well, and they delivered a baby boy. I was over the moon. I held the child in my arms and felt how special it was to have another son.

By now, the image of us as Bonnie and Clyde had run its course. We were not even that close anymore. I remember her once asking me: "Do you love me?"

I told her the truth, and said I did not know the meaning of love. "I am with you, and you are with me, because we each want a piece of someone else."

To me that meant it was all about sex, and the need to have your own home and a family, and therefore a wall of security around you. It was more to do with all those things.

Love was a totally unknown concept. I even believed it to be just a figment of people's imagination. What people thought of as love was in fact a confusion in their minds over a non-existent concept. It was in reality an addiction to a way of life, and simply another outlet for stimulation, either of the mind or of the body.

I thought of love as being like a dependency that gains strength through force of habit. From this habit came the possessive notion, the idea that one can control their environment, and own the person they live with—or at least believe they own her, and make attempts to own her.

The truth is that one cannot own another human being. It is an impossibility.

By now I was becoming a "bad ass." I was working on the coal truck earning wages, but I would also be filling extra bags with coal and selling them on the side. There was no sense of loyalty to my employer, nor any sense of a moral code, except the one that said that money took first place. I earned twice as much from my graft as I did from my official pay.

At that time I made friends with a man who owned two saluki dogs, which he used for deer hunting. He would sell the venison. This was illegal, and carried a penalty of eighteen months' imprisonment.

The danger made it all the more exciting, and all these activities would be carried out under the cover of darkness.

Typically, we would go to a place guarded by a game warden, and creep over the big walls of the country estate on the grounds of which the deer would be. Then we would bring the dogs over the wall.

We would creep through the woods and check to see if the game wardens were around. When we spotted the deer, we lit a lamp to shine at the deer. This dazzled them. The dogs would then run around the light beam and attack the deer. One of us would then cut the throat of the deer.

(No doubt a lot of people may find this as disgusting, as I now do.)

This friend was also the one who introduced me to the world of serious crime. He went around the country sussing out post offices and giving them a score from 1 to 10. Whichever P.O. had the lowest risk assessment, he would then "do" with his accomplice.

He gradually let me in on this as we began to get to know each other from our common interest in stalking deer. I would go with him on many such occasions.

One day, he came to me and asked me to help him with a problem he had with his partner in crime. They had done a post office and the alarm went off. They had to make a quick exit from the scene, cross-country. To have jumped back in the car and fled would have led to their being pulled over, as the roads were hot with police. So they trekked cross-country and buried their loot, about ten thousand pounds.

They always made sure they did banks the day before pensions were due. This was the time the safes would have the most money in them. Their strategy was to bury the money and escape quickly. They would then arrange to go back and recover the money when the heat had died down.

My friend went to this one site to collect the money, but found his accomplice had already been there and taken it himself. He got in touch with his accomplice and there was a scene about it. It turned out that his friend decided to do a slippery one with the money, and was not about to give him his share.

It was at this point that I came in. This was an opportunity for my ego to express itself, and to show my friend and his contacts how tough I really was. In my imagination, I wanted the world to perceive me as a notorious gangster.

The plan was for us to go and see his ex-accomplice, get him into the car, and basically scare the shit out of him. I was at the time in possession of a sawn-off shotgun.

As planned, we turned up on his ex-accomplice's doorstep. My friend knocked on the door. They had a few words, and I sat in the back of the car quietly as they both jumped in.

After a few words of encouragement, and with a little bit of a motivation from me sitting in the back with the sawn-off shotgun, the problem was hastily resolved. His ex-accomplice handed over his share of the money.

From that time on, I earned myself respect as someone who was willing to do what it needed to obtain money. I had "bottle," and had earned a ticket into the world of serious crime.

I BECAME MORE more convinced of the role I had created for myself. The tough-guy image gave one a lot of respect in the housing projects.

By now I had a feeling that sooner or later I was going to end up in prison. Everything was going wrong. I also became aware of a certain principle I had not acquired from book-reading. For everything I would gain in a bad way, something bad would come back to me. As they say today, "What goes around, comes around."

This was certainly true in my case. Whenever I ripped off some money, I would get a comeuppance one way or another, and these come-backs resulted in a very unhappy life. Still, I remained convinced that money meant happiness, and the more I had of it the better.

My relationship with Jayne had reached rock bottom. The violence was getting worse, and this was my own doing. I had decided I was not going to wear the skirt anymore.

One incident got really out of control. Once I had resolved that I was not going to let her win any more arguments, I had to do whatever was necessary to ensure this.

The usual happened, and we had a big row over nothing, and I was the culprit. Even my sanity was going down the chute. I did not care about the consequences of my actions any more. It was a kind of suicidal, devil-may-care attitude. That was how far I had gone down that road.

I cannot remember fully the details of the incident. When one gets in this state of mind, one loses the capacity to remember, as people sometimes do during a trauma.

My rage was so strong, and the emotions running so high, that after a lot of shouting and screaming I found myself holding the shotgun to her head and about to pull the trigger.

Then something strange happened. I felt as though I had been hit in the face with a blue light that was flashing on and off.

That snapped me out of it. I realized what was happening. I was seeing the flashing lights of a police car. We were standing in the bedroom, which was on the ground floor, and level with the road outside.

When I think about it now, I cringe, but if that police car had arrived one second later, I would have pulled the trigger and ended Jayne's life. It must have been divine intervention. We had many such arguments in the past, but why someone called the police for this one in particular, I will never know. Our arguments were a common occurrence, and the neighbors were used to us.

I was arrested and taken to a police cell. The shotgun was confiscated.

Now I am glad to have been spared. The guilt I would have had to live with for the rest of my life would have been unbearable. I would have been responsible not just for any murder, but for the murder of my son's mother. I could not have lived with it. But at that time I was going down a certain path, had something to prove, and was a very troubled young man.

My brother, John, turned up not long after this and asked me if I wanted to work with him. He was living in Manor Park, near London, and working in the West End of London.

I thought it would be an opportunity to get my head together, as I had been caught selling the extra bags of coal on the side and was fired. It was just coming up to Christmas, and I needed some money.

I had to quit the boxing training for the time being. It was difficult to train with all the pressure I was having from my domestic problems, even though after the last problem, things seemed to clear up.

Something had clicked inside Jayne, and she had changed for the better. She became a model mother and wife. There were no more temper tantrums or arguments. The demon had left her.

I guess it was the fear of looking down the loaded barrel of a shotgun with a madman at the other end of it, and the thought that this could have been her last day alive. The trauma must have affected her. She had never seen that rage in me before, and this had frightened the devil out of her.

The devil, though, had been activated in me. I had gone over the top, and did not know how to get back down.

The job in London turned up at the right time. I would be away from Jayne, and this would give me time to sort myself out.

I lived with my brother, worked, and paid them rent money that I had to force his wife, Terry, to accept. Since they would not take the money, I had to hide it some place she would later find it and not be able to return it. I stayed with them for some months. I would, though, go back to see Jayne on weekends.

On Fridays after work, it was our regular habit to go and have a drink in the pub with the other people who worked for the firm. This turned out to be not such a good idea. When John and I got together and the drink started to flow, there was always going to be trouble.

We were in our prime. John had been out of detention center for a few years, but while he was in there he had earned himself the title of the British lightweight Olympic lifting champion.

He was still a very powerful man with an explosive temper to match. I believe it was this explosive temper that had helped him win the championship. This was the same temper that got him banned from the Welsh schoolboy rugby team, when he had picked someone up and thrown the fellow to the ground, nearly breaking his back.

83

This takes a tremendous amount of explosive energy. With my brother John, that explosive energy came naturally. It was no wonder he was the ideal candidate for such a sport. Even as a child, he had a short fuse and was ready to erupt at any moment. When he was in school, some people would not walk down the same street as him for fear of his temper.

John and I together were a really bad combination. Many a time after a drinking bout, we would end up in conflicts with the odds stacked against us. (We would never take advantage of weaker people, though.)

On one such occasion, we had been drinking in the West End of London, and as usual I could not keep up with the drinking rounds. At the time, I needed only about three pints of beer, and that was my lot. I would, however, try to keep up with my brother, who could drink until the cows came home.

As the evening went by, I accumulated several rounds of drinks that my poor stomach could not accommodate. I was relieved when the barman called, "Time." However, my brother did not want to leave the pub until all the beers had been drunk. This meant we had to stay longer than the barman wanted us to.

The barman became impatient, my brother took a swing at him, and then all hell broke loose. It was me and my brother against ten or twelve of the staff.

We had a good thrashing. They stuck us in the middle of the pub and surrounded us. We were both covered in cuts, bruises, and our own blood, but I was fuming for more, even though I had already taken a beating. It stimulated in me the desire to fight on to the death.

My brother, wisely enough, thought better of it when I asked him: "Are you ready for some more?" We must have been a sight as we sat in the middle of the pub. Both of us had cut lips, swollen eyes, and bloodied noses.

The police turned up and arrested us.

We were taken to Bow Street Magistrates' Court. John had been in trouble some years before, and they had not been able to charge him at the time as he had done a disappearing act. They therefore took the opportunity to charge him with both crimes, and kept him in custody until the court date.

We went up for trial, and were given a three-month jail sentence, suspended for a year. To get in any more trouble would mean going to prison for three months, plus whatever time we received for the subsequent offense.

I now had to keep my nose clean, as did John. I thought this would be a good time to return home. Since I did not want to go to jail, it was better that John and I should part company.

Also, things seemed to be getting more and more out of control. I could not see that, after we had a couple of beers, that we were even going to remember that we had suspended jail sentences hanging over us.

Out of work and running short of money, I returned to Wales. If anything, I think the stay in London made me worse rather than better. My common-law wife, Jayne, loved the idea of me as the big tough guy. Whenever my brother and myself were to gather, to her we were the Kray twins.

This was yet another image to float around in my psyche, and another false identity to live up to.

I got back into the boxing again. Of course, now I was back with my old friend and we began to plan a job.

We were going to carry out an armed robbery.

WE HAD ALREADY done a safe. I was doing all I could to live up to an image that was in fact a figment of both my and other people's imaginations. Every day that went by I was turning this image into more and more of a reality. As I thought, so I became.

Although Jayne had become a much better person to live with, it was now my turn to go off the rails. I had lost all my understanding of right and wrong. For me, "right" meant my right to line my own pockets with gold, and "wrong" meant any situation where I did not get what I wanted. I was turning myself into my own god.

At the time I was collecting unemployment benefit. The officials pressured me into doing something toward gaining employment by threatening to cut off my benefits. I decided to do a six-month course as a bricklayer. I still believed that in due course I would be making a lot more money out of boxing, just as soon as I turned professional.

My brother would occasionally come visit. One time he turned up, we decided to go out on the town for a drink. It was a good opportunity to see him, as he lived so far away, and I did not see him often.

We went for a drink. We still had suspended jail sentences hanging over us, so we both had to be on our best behavior.

We went to a pub in Abersychan. John was really good to some old people in the pub that night, and bought them drinks. When I think about it, I was quite touched. He showed me an example of kindness that stayed with me for some time.

As the evening went on, the social niceties disappeared. John began to talk louder and louder, which attracted attention, as people in those small pubs always seem to talk in whispers. I did the same, and with the effects of the alcohol and forgetting where we were, a few swear words were let out.

At that, the barman asked us to kindly keep the swearing down. This ritual was then repeated.

My brother got up to go to the washrooms, and as he did I saw the barman walk toward him.

I knew straight away what was going to happen. Though I had had a few drinks, I was still very much aware that we were still on the suspended jail sentence.

I got up to stop what was about to happen, but I was too late. The barman said his bit, which I can only imagine, and then John let fly at him.

I tried to force myself to act sober, and had in mind that I could stop the incident from escalating into a full-fledged fight.

Suddenly, I got pulled over the top of my chair from behind. One of the regulars in the pub had taken it upon himself to intervene. He probably thought that I was going to start a fight with my brother, though that had not been my plan at all.

The next thing I knew, we were both bowled out of the pub. Outside, the barman and his loyal regulars muscled in on us.

Up to this point, I had been on the ground all the way through this scene, and did not have a chance to defend myself. As I stood up, I saw my brother with his back to the wall. I also had my back to the wall. The fight stopped momentarily.

Suddenly, John lashed out again. There must have been eight or ten people around us, all after a piece of our blood. I felt as though I had been pulled into something against my will, and was furious.

As soon as John lashed out at them, so did I. The barman took the brunt of it to begin with, but we were out-numbered and basically got beaten.

The police were called, and in due course I was taken to court for something that, as far as I was concerned, was not of my own instigation. In my mind, I was the aggrieved party. All I did was defend myself.

I was expecting to go to prison, but they gave me community service, which at that time was a new and experimental form of sentencing. They gave me the maximum penalty allowed, two sentences of 240 hours, to run concurrently. I avoided prison by the skin of my teeth.

The day we were in court, almost every landlord from every pub in and around Pontypool seemed to be there, either to learn who we were, or to pick up their liquor licenses. We were, as a result, banned from almost every pub in Pontypool and the surrounding area. What an achievement! I do not think that was a very common thing to happen in those days. I was not a regular drinker, so it did not bother me, nor John, as he lived in London anyway.

By now, the year of having the suspended sentence over me had elapsed, and though I had now been charged with more offenses and banned from every pub in the area, still I was not getting any better. On the contrary, I was getting more deeply involved in crime, and decided it was time to move on to even bigger things.

I was still boxing, and had won a few fights by now, and was getting ready for my first professional fight.

We were also planning our first big job. It was to be an armed robbery, and there was a lot of money at stake. We estimated it to be about thirty grand.

I had developed a cold and ruthless anger. I did not care about my own life, nor about the life of anyone else. Had I needed to, I would not have hesitated to blow someone away. I just did not care for any form of life.

From the child who had felt bad about sticking a metal spear into a dog that was already dead, I had become someone who would not think twice about sticking the same spear through a living human being.

There were two weeks to go before my fight, and another few weeks more before the job was to be carried out. It was getting close to Christmas.

We went down to Gosport to visit Jayne's family. We all had a drink, and before long all the family problems started to surface. Jayne had some problem with her brother, Mike. I stuck up for her, and the next thing, we were all outside fighting in their garden.

The fight spilled over on to the neighbor's property, and that brought him outside. By the time he came out, we had fallen over and were in a clincher on the ground. The neighbor was a burly fellow, very heavy, and he jumped on top of both of us.

Then Jayne came out and jumped on top of the neighbor. I was underneath all these bodies with my arm trapped in a very awkward position. It must have looked a sight to any onlookers. Christmas was coming, and what a way to party!

Under the pressure of the weight, my shoulder came out of joint. This was two weeks before my first pro fight. We went back home, but I was getting serious trouble with my shoulder. It kept coming out of joint.

Then my brother, John, turned up, and another fight somehow caused my other shoulder to come out of joint.

In the two weeks leading up to my first professional fight, I had managed to achieve something I had never in my life achieved before. I had managed to dislocate not one but both shoulders.

I had treatment for the dislocated shoulders, but they put an end to any ideas I had about turning professional. More than ever, this frustrated me. Looking back, it does seem as though those two shoulder dislocations happening at that time were the act of someone up there did not want me to be a pro boxer. He must have had other plans for me.

So there would be no more boxing. This was a hard thing to accept, as it was the only thing that was keeping me together. Boxing gave me hope that I was going to have something good for my future and for my children, and even more, to gain respect from other people. It seemed so important to prove myself.

Around that time, it was the fifth of November and bonfire night. They had arranged a fireworks display down at Pontypool Park.

I took the children down to see the fireworks. It was a freezing cold night, and we all put on extra clothing to keep warm. This was the first time for Phill, as he was only eighteen months old. Lee was about seven years old, and Richard was four.

I held Phill in my arms as the fireworks display started. I could see that Lee was enjoying himself. Phill was silently looking in awe at the display, and Richard was holding on to my leg as all the loud bangs and the sight of the fireworks display frightened him. He wanted to go home, so I had to reassure him it was okay. They were all three very different characters in their own right.

This was my last memory of my children, as what was to come next would take me away from them for a long, long time.

I HAD BY now become quite educated in the methods of determining what type of alarms are easy to deal with, which are fake, which are not, and of different ways to deal with the different types—how to disarm them, the different types of safes, which are easy to open, which are not so easy, and how to avoid leaving forensic evidence for the police to pick up.

I had a good teacher. My friend was well-established in his profession, and had many years of experience, including being caught, going to court, prison, and being held in police custody. He seemed to me quite switched on as criminals go, but in retrospect he could not have been that good at it, as he would get caught so many times.

Still, I was impressed. The time was getting closer for the job we planned—the big, make-or-break job.

My brother showed up again, as he always did. This time it was just days before we planned to do the job.

The police must have known something was about to happen. They had undercover officers pretending to do work on a telephone pole outside my friend's home. Every day, you would see a man up the pole, pretending to work. There was also a van parked just down the street with the windows blocked so no one could see inside.

When my friend first brought this to my attention, I thought he was becoming paranoid. As the days went by, however, it became obvious they were watching him. Why they made this so obvious beats me. Either they wanted him to know he was being watched, or they did not care if he knew. Perhaps the police were not all that skilful at the type of work they were doing, though I find that possibility hard to believe.

Their presence did not make me wary. Even though I knew what they were trying to do, it did not deter me from wanting to go ahead and do the job with him. He seemed so confident, and I went along with it. I was not dealing with my common-sense mind. The bigger part of my mind, the ego, had taken over.

We planned for every scenario. We arranged alibis, and people who were going to say where we were on the particular day we had chosen to carry out the heist. We felt it was a watertight plan.

The fact that the police were watching my friend so closely might even work to our advantage, as we could use the police themselves as an additional alibi.

Despite my confidence, I still had a strong feeling that I was somehow going to end up in prison quite soon. I was so sure of this that I began to ask people I knew who had been in prison what it was like, as if to prepare myself for the inevitable.

My brother, John, had warned me about this friend of mine. He told me he was a bad one who would end up getting me a prison sentence. Of course, John was quite accustomed to prison, but I was not. To him, prison was like being in his element. To me, it would be like being a wild bird with my wings clipped.

John told me to stop messing around with him, but being the arrogant person I was, this was not what my ego wanted to hear. I put it down to his jealousy. It was easier for me to see this in someone else than to see any wrong in myself.

Since my friend was at my house when my brother turned up, all three of us decided to go out for a drink. A year had now passed since we had been in the trouble with the pub, and this was our first night out since then. We made sure we did not go into the pub where the trouble had been. Instead, we went to a quiet pub not far away from it.

We bought a drink from of the young bar staff. I thought this was a good sign. Perhaps they did not know about us and the trouble we had been in twelve months previously just down the road.

As the barman walked in, I could see him looking over at us. I could read what was going on in his mind, and I knew he was not going to let us be served again.

My brother bought the first round, which was good. I knew that if he was refused, he would become agitated and lose his rag. More than likely he would take a swing at the barman. But we had not yet had enough to drink for that to happen.

When I went up to get the next round of beers, the staff refused to serve me. This was humiliating. In addition, I was still seething over what I saw as the unfairness of the previous incident.

That was it. They were not going to get away with treating me like that any more.

We all went home. We dropped my friend off, as I did not want him to be involved with what I was about to do. It was none of his business.

I told my brother I was going to make a bomb and stick it through the window of the pub where all this trouble had started a year earlier.

John looked at me, and I could see he did not believe me. But he could not be sure, because in all the years I had been his brother, he had never seen me like this before.

He decided to play along with me until, as he hoped, my bluff would be called. This was the attitude I picked up off him. He did not realize that I had changed inside over the last year, and become cold and callous. I am sure he did not believe that I meant every word I said.

I made the bomb, and obtained a mask, so that no one could see my face when I threw the bomb through the pub window. Then I found some old army clothes and put them on. I took a spare set of clothes to change into once I had planted the bomb. My plan was to burn the set of old army clothes to destroy any forensic evidence of explosives.

We got in John's car. I could see he was still thinking I would not do it. I arranged for him to drop me off at a spot where I would not be witnessed either leaving or returning to the car.

I got out, and made my way uphill toward the pub. The window was just at the top. I pulled the mask over my face, lit the bomb, and lobbed it through the window.

As the bomb went through the window, I could see a stream of fire go straight across the bar room. I quickly ran into my brother's car, where he sat waiting for me.

He was speechless and hurriedly drove us away. We went to an isolated spot where I burned my old army clothes and put on the clean set. Then we went back home and I took a bath.

I informed Jayne and John what to say if the police showed up. As long as we all stuck to the same story, we would be okay.

About an hour went by and there was a knock on the door. A policeman came in, asked us a lot of questions, and read us our rights.

Then they took us away for questioning. As we went get into the police car, John's flight instinct got the better of him. He made a run for it and the police gave chase. For several days he trekked across country to avoid them. They could not catch him, though. In his younger days he had a lot of experience of being on the run. Whenever the police arrested him, he would always run if given half a chance. He responded to his instincts and experience, and successfully escaped.

I, on the other hand, was kept in a police cell for three days while they questioned me about the incident. I kept my mouth shut and did not answer any of the questions they grilled me with. They took all my clothes for forensic tests. I knew I would come up clean, as they were not the clothes I used for the bombing. The only thing I asked, as they do in the movies, was to see my lawyer. Those were the only words I would speak until my lawyer showed up.

I believe I had been in custody in the police cell for two days by the time the lawyer came. The first thing he said to me was: "It looks very bad for you."

The lawyer suggested the best thing for me to do, in the light of all the evidence they had against me, was to throw myself at their mercy. "Tell them everything, and we may be able to make a deal to reduce your sentence," he said.

On my third day in custody, on the advice of my lawyer, I made a statement admitting that I had done the crime, and giving them a story which was close to the way I had actually done it. I purposely included some inaccuracies as a kind of safety net, in case I later changed my mind.

Then I was taken to Cardiff prison remand wing, and put in a cell with two other inmates.

The conditions were cramped. The cell had room for one double bunk bed, one single bed, one table, and one chair. Only one person could stand up at any one time.

In the corner was a bucket in case you needed to relieve yourself. The bucket threw up a revolting smell, and to top it off, one of the inmates was unfamiliar with the concept of personal hygiene. Between the smell of this inmate and the smell of the bucket it was like living in a cesspit. Still, I deserved what I got.

No one was hurt in the incident, I finally found out. At the time, though, I was more worried about myself than anyone else. I was still cold in my feelings toward others, and only cared about me, mine, and the possibility of a prison sentence.

The charges were arson and attempted murder. Attempted murder on its own can carry a life sentence. That was what I was looking at in addition to the arson charge. I was in serious shit.

Every seven days, I was sent under escort to Pontypool Magistrates' Court by the prison screws (guards) to appeal for bail. With a serious crime like this, though, there was not a chance in hell of getting bail.

The only thing good about the situation was that I was close enough to home for Jayne to come and visit me. The least sentence I was told to expect was seven years, and I told Jayne this on one occasion when she came.

In my heart, I knew she would not wait that long, and I told her I did not expect her to wait for me. She assured me, though, that she would wait for me. I suppose this made me feel secure. Though we never had a good relationship, it was all I had ever known, and the only thing I had going for me in life.

I had strong feelings about my young children growing up without knowing me. I wanted to be their father in a real way. I could not handle the thought of them being raised by someone else.

Besides getting a visit once a week, I would get at least one or two letters from Jayne every week. It was not long after I had told her to expect a long sentence that I had a letter from her saying she was feeling ill, and that she had been to the doctor.

This was the last time I heard from her. I wrote her saying that I had discovered that my lawyer had given me false information about the possibility of appealing for leniency. Basically, he had stitched me up with the police.

In fact, the only evidence the police had against me was my own statement, and the fact that we had been seen in the general area of the pub on the night of the bombing. I retracted my statement, and decided to plead not guilty. One thing that looked bad was the fact that my brother had done a runner, but this was not conclusive proof that I was involved in the bombing.

I mentioned all this in my letter to her, and thought I was telling her good news. I asked her to come and stand up for me in the witness box, and make a statement. It would, of course, have been a false statement to cover my ass.

Jayne did not reply straight away. Then one day I got a letter from her saying she had been diagnosed with cancer.

This blew my mind. She also said she was not going to stand up in court and tell a load of lies for me.

After this, I never heard from Jayne again. I only heard about her through people coming into prison from the area where we lived. Once, I was told that she was with living another man, but I would not accept this. Then I was told she had left the house where we used to live, but I could not accept this, either.

One day, I was taken on a police visit, and the detective questioned me about an electricity meter. He said my common-law wife had been ripping off the electricity company.

This was, in fact, something I had taught her how to do. The electricity company had obviously contacted the police. Jayne told the police it was me who had tampered with the meter, and I took the blame in order to take the heat off her. At that point I thought she had cancer, and that perhaps she might now get in touch with me, but still I did not hear from her.

The rumors about her having a new partner became more frequent. Again, I was told she was with another man.

I became very angry, and decided I was going to break out of prison. If what I had heard was true, I was going to kill her for that. There was no way she was going to get away with this. She had totally let me down, and I was going to make sure she paid for it.

Jayne's brother turned up in Cardiff prison at the time I was there. He was on his last few weeks of sentence, and I told him to tell her what I was going to do, and that nothing was going to stop me.

I noticed that when the prison screws would hand me over to the police for bail appeal, they would take off the handcuffs just before they handed me over. Normally I would be without handcuffs at the point I was taken from the cells up to the dock.

This was my opportunity to escape. I would only have to get past two or three police officers and through two doors, and then I would be out on the street. To make my escape, I would also have to climb a ramp around the other side of the police station. From there, I was going to head for the railway track and make my way to freedom.

The day came for me to be taken to Pontypool Magistrates' Court for my bail plea and to make my planned escape. As usual, they took me into the administrative part of the police station and removed the handcuffs. As luck would have it, there was only one police officer between me and the door I had to run through.

I waited until the prison guards had signed me over and left, and then I made my dash for the door.

This caught them by surprise. I got through one door successfully, then I made it through the outer door on to the street.

I sprinted with all my might. I knew if I could quickly put some distance between myself and the police, I could get into running mode, pace myself, and run for hours.

Because I was so fit, no one would be able to catch me if I could only make the gap. This was the most important thing to do. I put every ounce of effort into making a gap between me and my pursuers.

I got around the side of the building and on to the ramp leading to a parking garage. I had made a good distance by this point.

Dashing up the ramp to the parking garage, I was halfway along when a group of people got on to the ramp from the parking end. They took up all the available space, and I was going to have a problem getting past them.

I looked down and saw the police coming around the side of the police station. I could not go back the way I came, as they would catch me. Looking over the side of the ramp, I realized it was too high to jump down without injuring myself.

My only hope was to see if I could break through the group of people who had come on to the ramp. I had no other choice.

As the group got closer, I could see one big fellow. He stood out from the rest. Suddenly he stuck out his arms and grabbed me. That was all I needed—a bloody do-gooder.

We struggled, and the struggle gave the police enough time to catch up with me. They overpowered me and took me back into custody.

At the time, I thought the fellow that had done this was a complete asshole, but now I am grateful that he was put in my path. If I had escaped at that point, I might never have come to where I am today. And, as events were about to prove, prison would be the best thing that happened to me.

TAKEN BACK TO Cardiff prison, I was put in an "e-man" cell. That meant that, as an escapee, you required higher security. You lost all the privileges that regular remand prisoners have.

One thing I was glad about was that it also meant I had a cell to myself, and did not have to put up with the stench from living with two other inmates.

I was banged up for twenty-three hours of the day. If it was raining and impossible to exercise outside, I was locked up twenty-four hours of the day.

We were segregated from all the other inmates. When I was on normal remand, there was quite a lot of freedom. You had a lot of association time, and your cell door was open quite a lot, so you could move around. Even when they shut the door, there was always something to do.

Now all I had was this cell space and a door locked for twenty-three or twenty-four hours of the day.

I had always been used to being able to come and go whenever I had pleased. Now suddenly I could not. I had a lot of energy, and there was no way of using it up.

Despite the loss of privileges, my mind was still pre-occupied with the idea of escape. I would not give up this easily—not as long as I had breath in my body.

I investigated the cell and its brickwork. With all the time on my hands, I could examine every part of it. I noticed a weak point. There was an air vent that was big enough to squeeze a body through. The question was, how to take out the bricks and mortar without being noticed.

Saturdays were the day we all went to the prison cinema. Maybe it was fate, but this particular Saturday, before my escape attempt, the movie was about a con named McVicar. He was in prison and made an escape in the movie. He took out the brickwork, but the most ingenious thing was how he avoided detection.

McVicar had the free privilege of being allowed watercolor paints and paper mache. He replaced the brickwork with the paper mache and then painted over it with the watercolors so that it blended in with the remaining brickwork. No one could tell the difference.

My escape plan was thus borrowed from watching a movie in prison, about a prisoner who successfully escapes from prison!

All I needed now was a tool to help remove the bricks. Again, I looked at everything in the cell, and inspected the way the bed was made. It was put together loosely from heavy pieces of metal. The bolts were loose, so all I had to do was unbolt the bed, then use the bottom end like a sledge hammer. Because it was made of heavy metal, I just had to hold it by one leg while I used the other to hit the brickwork.

It was a totally brilliant tool. In no time, I obtained some water-color paints and paper mache, and began working on my escape.

I figured the best time to make my break would be when all the working prisoners were taken to their jobs. Most of them had jobs within the prison. During the day, I could make as much noise as I liked, because all the guards would be elsewhere, and any sound I made would be put down to some other activity, especially if heard from a distance.

I started my first day, and it went well. Because the legs of the bed were so heavy, they shifted the brickwork quite nicely. All I had to do then was to remove the outside bricks. My plan was to get out into the yard and scale the wall.

There were buildings close to the wall I wanted to scale, and I had blankets I could use as rope. After I stopped working on this project at the end of the first day, I realized I had done much more than I thought possible. By next day, I would have a hole right through the prison wall to the outside world. Just one more day, and one more night, and I would be out.

I began to feel nervous about crossing the yard and scaling the wall. If my timing was right, I would have no problem. And this was no time to start thinking in a negative way. That would only make another failed attempt at escape. I had to keep a positive and focused mind, without any thoughts of, "If I get caught."

The next day, I woke up and did the usual routine of slopping out, followed by breakfast. Then the prison guards took the regular prisoners to their day jobs.

But this morning when the door opened to slop out, a prisoner I had seen occasionally on the landing came into my cell.

With a half-hesitant look on his face, he said: "Look I don't know anything about you, or who you are, but I thought this must be important for you. I had a dream last night. I saw you climbing

99

out of the prison cell. Then you got down to the prison yard, and you were captured by the prison guard dogs and torn up."

I looked at him and the expression on his face was serious.

Then he turned and left, having said nothing else. He was an ordinary young man, maybe mid-twenties or younger. I looked at the hole in the wall, and there was nothing to prove to anyone what I was doing. How could he have seen this in a dream?

I did not know, but I felt it was a warning. I always believed that there was something that looked after me. If the dream was a warning, then from whom? How could he have known? I had told nobody of my plans.

These considerations put a stop to that idea of escape.

I also became aware of something I had not experienced since I was a child.

I was claustrophobic.

Stuck in that cell, I would freeze up, and tension would grip my body. If I tried to keep still, my body would physically shake. It only seemed to stop after dark, when the sun had set for the day.

The only way I could deal with the claustrophobia was to pace up and down the cell in a figure-of-eight, all day long, until the sun went down.

The only thing I had in the cell with me was a Bible the prison chaplain must have left. There was nothing else, just myself and my own mind, which by now was well screwed up.

I contemplated suicide, and all manner of negative things, as I paced up and down the cell in a figure-of-eight. This went on for some days. I was coming to a point where I decided I was going to do something drastic.

Every day I was waking up with a screwed-up belly. There was a knot of hatred in there—hate for the people who were supposed to stand by me, and who had let me down, especially my common-law wife, Jayne.

I wondered what had happened to my children. Where were they? Would I ever see them again? I thought not, as my mind by now was so totally focused on hate and resentment.

I had to do something, and soon.

Finally, one day, I remembered an article I had once read in a magazine about meditation. The article said you could mediate and find peace.

I was aware that, though I had so many negative feelings running through me and consuming my thoughts, this was not the right way to live.

That article had aroused my curiosity, and I decide to give meditation a go. It was either that, or if I carried on thinking the way I was, I would have topped myself.

This in itself gave me a strong motivation to learn how to meditate. I would make my escape not through the prison walls but through my mind.

❧ *8* ❧

Learning to Meditate

MY FIRST ATTEMPT at meditation was a somewhat feeble try. It was still daylight, and I sat down in what I remembered was called the lotus position. The article said it was important to maintain an erect spine, since the spine supported all the nerves vital to the functioning of the body's nervous system.

It was a pretty poor attempt. It was still daylight, and the feeling of freezing up was so strong I could not last longer than five minutes. It seemed more like five hours to me.

I could not get back on my feet fast enough, and went back to pacing up and down the cell in a figure-of-eight. There was a freedom in the pacing, since it dissipated the pent-up energy I could release in no other way. As I paced, my mind now had something to focus on other than my hate and anger.

It is a common experience when exercising that the longer you stick it out, the easier it becomes to last a bit longer the next time. Also, I was strongly motivated to live, for whatever my life it was worth. Perhaps I was too much of a coward to commit suicide, but that was my only other way out of this situation, as I was looking at a long stretch of a prison sentence.

I decided that the next time I meditated, I would try and hold out longer than five minutes. Hopefully I would obtain the same increase in staying power you experience when exercising. The more you persevere, the less the resistance next time. My aim was for ten minutes.

I sat down in the lotus position again. This time I lasted six to eight minutes. Again, the freezing and shaking that gripped me were intense.

Also, I noticed a fear. It was the fear of being stuck in this one position and holding it for any length of time. I knew this was not normal, and that I had to get over it.

Back on my feet, I started to pace again. I was disappointed with myself to the point of depression. I experience the same result on the next few attempts. By now, I thought I should be getting in at least ten minutes.

At least I had been able to observe my mind, and what was going on. It was like a whirlwind of thoughts running from one subject to another at random, as if driven by whatever the weather was doing at the time, and with no intelligent oversight.

The fact is, my mind was like a garbage heap.

Thoughts centering on all my wants, all the people I hate, all my hopes, my future, what I want for the future, my fears, how to counter my fears, what lies to tell to get things to go right for me, constant replays of things that have happened, how I like or dislike the end of the scene in some past episode, how I would re-enact the scenario in case of a similar event happening in the future, how I want it to turn out for me if I have to deal with it again, how I would set anyone right for my own aggrandizement, how I could get my own back, and if I could not, then more hatred in my stomach, because they were being allowed to get away with acting against me, and it wasn't right that they should get away with it!

These thoughts seemed never-ending. They were so ingrained into my way of using my thinking faculties that this seemed natural for me. But the truth was, it was out of control.

There was something seriously wrong. This could not be right—to keep feeling like this all the time. The hatred was lodged in my stomach, and every day I would wake up and feel it, as if it were a real physical object lodged in my stomach.

It did not make me feel good. It was interfering with my eating. I could not smile; there was a feeling of a sickness about it. Despite the fact that I wanted to feel good, I could not.

So I blamed it on all those people who had done me wrong. Surely, that was what it was, and where the fault lay. This was why I felt like this.

It was not my fault. It was outside my control. The reason I was here was because I got pulled into a fight I did not want. I had only protected myself. As far as I was concerned, they deserved what I had done to their pub.

That put it all in perspective. As they had done wrong to me, so I did wrong to them. This should not have happened to me, since I was in the right.

I secretly knew that I had gone over the top, but my need to justify what I had done was stronger than my reasoning. I was not going to let reasoning enter into my thinking about the situation. It was other people who made me like this. It was nothing to do with me—or was it?

Every day I practiced the meditation. When I became aware of the state my mind was in, it gave me even more determination to persevere, and deal with it properly.

I had read somewhere it was possible to stop the mind from thinking, and this became my aim. If another human being was capable of such a feat, then so was I.

Through sheer determination, the length of my meditations began to increase. Soon I was up to a half-hour at a time. Then, after meditating, I would as usual pace up and down the cell.

As I walked, I glanced at a brand-new Bible left on top of the table. It was called *The New English Bible*.

I was never one to read very much, and my standard of education was not very high. I had barely learned to read and write by the time I left school. When I had the simplest of tests to get in the army, I passed only because of the help of the recruitment sergeant who had taken a liking to me.

The thought of sitting down to read a whole book had been, up until that point, totally out of the question. I could sit down and read small articles. But to read a whole book?

Still, I felt a strong pull to find out about the Bible. This pull went back many years. I had always wanted to find out what was written in this book, but had never had the time. Now that I had the time, I did not know how. Yet the pull was so strong!

When I had been at Snatchwood Junior School, every morning at assembly the headmaster would read a story from the Bible. He started off at Genesis, in the Old Testament, and continued each story in daily installments. He would miss out parts of a sexual nature, though the Bible does makes quite a few references to sexual matters in the Old Testament.

I remembered listening to the stories of King David and his band of heroes and all their conquests. There were stories of bravery and great friendships, of Samson and Delilah, and of this God who would do fantastic things.

One story I remembered was the story of young Samuel, who was raised in the temple of God. One day, he heard God call his name. He told the old man Eli this, and was instructed that the next time he heard his name called, he should say: "Speak, Lord, for your servant is listening" (1 Samuel 3:9).

Hearing that this happened to Samuel, and remembering that this very same thing had happened to me when I was younger and living up Garndiffaith, had a strong impact on me. I had always felt a presence with me—a presence that was always watching me, even correcting me and punishing me if I did wrong, just like in those stories in the Bible. Was this the God the Bible had spoken about doing all these things to me?

Many a time these thoughts crossed my mind as I paced up and down my cell. The Bible caused me to question what it was that had spoken to me as a child. I had thought it was my father. But was it God? Or what?

At this point, I made a new plan. I would carry on with the meditating and then, still in the hours of daylight, I added another challenge. After meditating, I would sit down and read my way through the Bible.

It started more or less the same way as the meditating. At first it was just a few minutes. As time went by, I built it up to last a bit longer, until I was spending about a half-hour meditating followed by ten minutes' Bible-reading.

Unfortunately I then went through a phase when I became disillusioned with the promises that meditation had offered. I could not see any significant changes in my thinking patterns, nor any sign of this supposed peace and calm. The only difference was the fact that I could now actually sit down during daylight hours. I suppose this was an achievement for me, but in comparison to other people, it meant nothing. It was just a bit below normal.

And it is true that I could also sit down and read, which for me was also an achievement, though my reading abilities were subnormal compared to the average person.

When I realized this, I decided to put even more effort into my self-assigned tasks. Any time I felt weak or incapable, I resolved to become even determined. If most of the population could do this, then so could I.

That determination gave me a new influx of energy toward reaching my aim. The determination was also driven by emotion, and specifically from feelings of hopelessness. Others could do this but I could not. Why not? What was wrong with me?

A conception of myself as being a kind of invalid hit quite deep, and stirred up a newfound energy within me, a kind of angry determination.

I resolved to myself: "I am going to succeed!"

* * *

I NOW COMMITTED myself to sticking out the meditation for longer periods of time. I really wanted to succeed in my quest, to conquer this dilapidated mind of mine, and to get on top and in control.

I sat down and pushed past the half-hour mark. The first difficulty I had was being able to keep my body still and to resist the temptation to scratch, or to move into a more comfortable position. This was a task in and of itself.

With effort, I learned to overcome this hurdle. I would come to a point where I would feel pain in my body, and in particular in my back. The muscles would ache, and again I would want to move.

This was indeed a battle.

I made it, and my meditations began to last as long as an hour. My Bible-reading periods were also lasting that long. I was beginning to relax. I did not need to pace up and down so much. My quality of sleep was improving, too, and I would wake up feeling refreshed in the mornings.

My concentration span became longer. Before, I had a concentration span of about ten minutes, but now it was more like forty-five minutes. I became convinced that this meditation was beginning to help me. This conviction gave me even more enthusiasm to keep going, and to ignore any thoughts I had of quitting.

Though I was meditating now for about an hour, I was always aware of what was going on around me. I had read about reaching this state called a trance, but there was no way I had achieved that state of mind yet.

I realized, too, that the idea of the training principle had been right. That was proven to me, because now I was meditating for an hour at a time, and it was no longer a struggle.

My next aim was to reach a trance state, if indeed there was such a state to reach. When I would come out of the one-hour meditations, I would occasionally look around the cell and think: "Back here again in this hole." It seemed as if there was a certain freedom in meditation, and I felt so good doing it.

I also noticed that the thoughts in my mind were slowing down. There did not seem to be so much of a tornado inside my head. But though they were slowing, the thoughts had not yet stopped.

Was it really possible to stop your thoughts? If it was possible, I was going to do it. Looking at the cell walls, I saw I was not in the best position in the world, but if I could get out of it by meditating, then it was worth a try.

I worked even harder at keeping the meditations going longer. All the time, I was feeling better and better in myself. The Bible-reading, too, was becoming a valuable part of my day.

In the Old Testament I had been reading about how God would treat the Israelites for their wrongdoings. I saw the pattern of behavior that would lead the Israelites to experience what is called "God's wrath" in the Bible. Story after story told how they would go through periods where they committed sin, and then return to the teachings of Moses and the Ten Commandments, and how God would then take care of them. Then they again slowly stopped practicing the Ten Commandments, and God's wrath would cause things to go pear-shaped, and bad things would happen to them.

Looking back at all the things that I had done, I could easily empathize with this situation, and then gradually I became aware of how I had never really gotten away with anything that was morally unjust.

Seeing this actually written down in the Bible, and confirming it in my own experience, convinced me that there was some kind of universal law in operation. You cannot take from the universe what does not belong to you, and not have to pay in one way or another.

In the religions of India they call this the law of karma. What-ever one wishes to call it, it certainly exists. I am now convinced that everyone should actively try to understand this, and live life in awareness of this law of the universe.

The meditation got to a critical point. Whenever I meditated past the hour mark, although I had overcome the desire to move into a more comfortable position, or scratch part of my anatomy, there was also a point where my mind would get caught up in a chain of thinking. The chain would carry me away from the task I had set myself, which was the complete annihilation of thinking.

As I got caught in the chain of thinking, it would crystallize into a dream-like state, similar to that which one experiences when one falls asleep and dreams. Instead of being aware of meditating, I became a participant in the dream and totally lost in it. Usually, since I was seated in the lotus position, my head would suddenly drop forward and wake me out of the dream. Then I would re-focus myself on the task of emptying my mind.

As I continued to meditate, I found certain problems and thoughts were so strong they would not go away, not for love nor money. I decided the next time these problems or thought-patterns came up, I would became aware of them *as they emerged*.

I discovered these persistent thoughts were triggered from the mind, but hooked into the emotional feeling center. This is why they were so hard to get rid of.

These types of chained thoughts (a patterned, well-rehearsed chain of associated thinking) did not allow me to remain in the position of being the watcher of these thoughts. Instead, I would repeatedly become lost in them.

It was as if in this type of thinking my mind was a mechanical dream-making engine. Once it has been started, it took on a life of its own that allowed no variation in its motion. It was limited to following its own program, defeating the purpose of the meditation.

Thoughts tied with strong emotions are the most difficult to learn to deal with. The best solution, when they arise, is to stay with the difficult feelings. The reason they were there was because I was not dealing with them properly in everyday life, and so when I went to sleep, or into the meditation, they hit me full force.

They had to be dealt with. In dealing with these types of

thoughts, my first consideration was: "I do not want to feel like this." The next point was: "What is causing this? Is it the way I am thinking? Is it wrong?"

I had to accept there was indeed something wrong with the way I was thinking. A healthy person should not, and does not, have to suffer in this way. It is not right.

I asked myself: Can anything be changed for the better by thinking like this? Definitely not. From where, then, do I start? Well, I thought, first I have to get rid of that horrid feeling and negative emotion that is so intimately connected with those thoughts.

My strategy was to focus on whichever thought created the most negative feeling—the one that really made me react in a bad way. I examined what might be a whole cluster of thoughts until I found the one with the strongest reaction and strongest emotions in my feeling center.

Then I would intentionally "think" the problematic thought, and feel its effects in the pit of my stomach, even though I did not really want to think that thought as it was the source of so much emotional pain.

At this point, then, I had to discipline myself to stay with it. I wanted to get it out of my mind. After all, it was hurting me. But like a cowboy at a rodeo, I resolved to stay on the back of it, no matter what.

Nothing would be sorted out if I kept running away because I did not like the way it was making me feel. If I ran, the hurt would be just that much more next time, like a bad tooth. It has to be dealt with sooner than later. And just like a bad tooth, if left untreated, it can poison the whole system.

So I had to find a way to deal with these thoughts. If I did not, I was only kidding myself that I was doing proper meditation, or that it was really doing me any permanent good.

I learned to be ready and waiting when these thoughts arose. Like needy little children, they would return if not happy with what they were given the first time. What followed then was a process of elimination.

One of strongest reactions, the one I had worst reaction to, was the thought of my wife having sex with another man. This would be followed by vivid and disturbing images in my mind. My strongest reaction was to the image of her in the arms of another man.

As I stayed with it, and delved into it, I felt anger arising in my feeling center. I then put myself through a question-and-answer process to resolve the issue. It would go something like this.

Q. Why am I feeling angry?

A. I am angry because my wife is with another man, and she has let me down.

Q. But why? Where does this anger come from within me?

A. It comes from the middle of my stomach. It is a feeling that does not feel good.

Q. Where does it start? Does it actually start in the stomach?

A. It starts from the thought in my mind of her being with another man. These thoughts then make my stomach feel this way; they have to be wrong for me.

Q. Why?

A. Because I do not feel right. I feel like I want to kill because of them, and that is not right.

Q. Why do you want to kill?

A. Because she belongs to me and no one else.

Q. Does she really belong to you?

A. We are common-law husband-and-wife. She belongs to me.

Q. But that is not right. How can you really own another human being? What is written on paper is not what is for real. How can you own another flesh-and-blood being like yourself? What is ownership?

A. Ownership is what I have worked hard for, and it belongs to me.

Q. As if she were a robot. You think she is a part of you because you own her, do you? She does everything you say, then does she? Has she not got a mind of her own? Does anyone own you, and have you done everything they say to you, as if you were their robot?

A. No, she is not a robot, she is a human being like myself, and I guess that in that context, no, I cannot own anyone. And yes, she has her own mind, like myself. No, I would not accept anyone trying to own me, or telling me how to run my life.

Q. What then do you think it is like in her position? Is she having a whale of a time?

A. No, she cannot be having a very good time of it, as she was dependant on me, and now I am not there, and we have three sons to look after. She has to pay all the debts and the expenses for the upkeep of the house.

Q. Who has the rawest deal? She, who is outside struggling to survive because you let her down by going to prison, or you who have only your own mind to deal with, and no responsibility?

A. She has the rawest deal, I guess, as she has to survive on her own with three young children.

Q. How would you react if you were in her shoes?

(At this point of the meditation, I had to be realistic and put myself into her position. I used visualization and imagination and managed to become totally unbiased, taking into consideration all her strengths and weaknesses. I had to totally forget myself before I gave the next answer. It takes time, and I had to lose my identity and concern for self in order to get a totally unbiased and true answer. Also, I had to understand Jayne, and feel exactly as she must have felt. In truth, we are all the same. Everyone is just trying to find their own happiness, and sometimes mistakes are made, and a price has to be paid for those mistakes. Essentially, we are all looking for happiness, but in different shapes and forms.)

A. Yes, I understand why she is doing this. It is because, like me, she is weak, and if I were in her shoes, as I now understand them, I would also try to find a way out, even though the amount of choice she has is very limited, since she is a weak person. So am I. She took what she thought was an easier way, to make her life better. Now I also understand why she put the children in a home.

It must have been a very difficult and hard thing for her to do, and she must be really hurting inside as this was a very extreme thing to do, and to feel that she had to do it, I can only say that her hurt must run deeper than mine—much, much, deeper, and she must be a very mixed-up person, and all this was because of me. It was my initial action that caused her to react; if I had not done that, then none of this would have happened.

Q. What right, then, have you to expect any better of her?

A. I have no right whatsoever, and now I only wish her well, and that things will get better for her, and for our children. I hope that one day I will put right all the wrongs I have done, if I am ever given the chance. To do that, I must wait till I am out of prison. As it is right now, I have no power to affect anything except my own my mind.

ASTONISHINGLY, THE NEGATIVE feelings now reversed poles. They changed from what had been bad feelings—hatred and resentment toward Jayne, and blaming her for my hurt—to feelings of compassion and understanding; a wanting things to be better for her, who was now suffering because of me and my wrongdoing. This, then, created in me the platform needed to go further in my life and in my meditation.

A large hurdle had been surmounted. I was ready to take the next step forward into progressively deeper meditation. I had learned that thoughts create feelings, and feelings can create thoughts. During the process of thought development, a permanent link can be formed between thoughts and feelings, thus creating an automatic chain of responses. The responses, when made for the first time, are made from awareness. However, over time they become automatic, almost as if running a piece of computer software.

Early in life, we learn specific responses to feelings in the stomach created by some external stimulus. For example, stamping one's feet is socially unacceptable among adults. So, instead of stamping one's feet at the creator of a negative external stimulus, the adult learns to respond in a socially-acceptable way. Rather then demonstrate anger openly, the adult hides it, and finds an appropriate alternative response that demonstrates the anger in a controlled, socially acceptable manner. Rather than responding physically, the response may be a counter-threat which, taken on the face of it, may even appear to be concern for the other person. An example of such a response might be: "If you continue to do such and such, you might run into someone who will take offense, and really lay into you."

By the time one has reached adulthood, these emotions and responses become inseparably linked, even though the learned response no longer has any relation to the actual emotional feeling. Over the years, one can become oblivious to one's real emotional feelings, and not recognize their language. Habits are formed in the same was as water running down the side of a mountain for many years will eventually become ingrained into the landscape of the mountain. This is how it is with responses to the emotional feeling center.

I had to work on my feeling center by learning to know what it was truly saying, and becoming more truthful, first to myself, and then to others. I notice now that many people do not know the language of the feelings. At that point, neither did I.

It is so common to become detached and unaware of our true feelings. Instead of openness and honesty with ourselves and others, we automatically voice sentiments that social convention has taught us are appropriate reactions.

This perpetuates a continued lack of awareness of what we really feel. Our true feelings remain submerged, causing difficulties for ourselves and others when, unrecognized, they emerge in our interactions with others.

A simple example will illustrate the point. A wife meets up with an old male friend from her school days, and they make a lunch date to talk over old times. When the husband accidentally finds out about the plan, rather than expressing the jealousy he really feels, he plans lunch with his wife at precisely the same time, and then claims he had no knowledge of her conflicting plans. He may even convince himself that he forgot about her other plans.

This passive-aggressive ploy allows the husband to achieve his goal without dealing with his true feelings, and without the appearance or blame that attaches to "the jealous husband."

When we realize that the mouth is speaking something disconnected from the real feelings, this is a sign that we have hidden negative emotional feelings we do not want other people to know about. It also signifies that these feelings have become suppressed because of an early negative experience associated with them.

The work of meditation is to recognize suppressed emotions and to root them out, rather than allowing them to remain submerged in the psyche.

If feelings are allowed to remain submerged, our lives are like a chariot pulled by horses without a charioteer having control over the horses. The horses represent feelings. The charioteer is the mind.

If the charioteer does not take the reins, the horses take the charioteer wherever they please. The terrain may vary from pleasant to rough, but eventually the chariot will be overturned.

If on the other hand the charioteer learns to hold the reins and guide the horses, the journey through life becomes joy and bliss.

Once aware of what the feelings are saying, the mind will recognize its own truth, and become a valuable tool for visualization, imagination and creation. An aware, disciplined mind is a valuable asset, just as the undisciplined, uncontrolled mind can be a source of much unhappiness.

It is important that we dig into ourselves right down to the roots of the problem until we totally understand what has happened to us and what its effects on us were. If we have a recurring problem that will not leave us alone, we need to accept it, analyze it, and defuse it, by seeing that it is due to a wrong way of thinking. If we deal with all problems in this way, we will realize they are all due to wrong ways of thinking.

Moreover, we cannot understand another's hurt until we understand our own. It is only our own pain that allows us to recognize how others feel. Blaming others for our own perceptions creates a kind of deadlock—a negative energy circulating internally creating both physical and emotional problems.

By analyzing the problem correctly, and attributing it to our way of thinking, we balance ourselves with positive energy. This is both emotionally and physically beneficial. Our energy is restructured into empathy and compassion, which are good medicine for both body and mind. We have gone full circle, and come back a better, fuller person.

I also found that dealing with problems in this way—re-polarizing energy—creates positive energy that energizes the body. Have you noticed how problems drain the life-force away from you in the form of depression, tiredness and lethargy?

From this process of dealing with problems, or what I identified as problems, I also became aware of what a liar I had been to myself and the world. Underneath all the pretense was the belief that I was not a good person. Up until that point, I had not been even slightly aware of this. I had been pretending to be something I was not feeling inside.

At this point in my meditation, I began to ask why I was like I was. From where, and at what time in my life, did all these unnatural, ingrained responses come? Why did I have a particular reaction to particular external events?

To do this investigation, I would bring to mind an event to which I had attached strong thoughts and feelings. I would then sit listening to my feeling center, totally focused on the feelings in the solar plexus area of my stomach.

Quite often, my response did not match what I was actually feeling. For example, I would experience jealousy in the feeling center, but my response would be one that would make me look good. The response was one that would not have a negative backlash that a true response made out of jealousy would bring about.

I came to recognize all these bad habits in myself and worked on them each in turn.

Dealing with myself in this way, after some time and effort, allowed the emergence of a new sensation in my feeling center. What was once hatred turned into compassion for others.

Whenever a bad feeling was there, I asked why, and where it came from, and I would be transported back in time to the event and the place where the response had originated.

Often I had to rip down false self-images that lay behind these responses in order to see why I was holding on to an idea that was so obviously wrong.

If the event happened at a time when I was not in possession of a good reasoning mind, more often than not, the reaction developed from a wrong attitude—an attitude which would not allow anyone to perceive me as weak. I always wanted to be perceived as strong.

This, then, was how I learned everything about myself—through relentless self-inquiry.

I learned the reason for every development in my life. I learned where all the good things and all the bad things came from.

There were many more bad than good things. I asked myself if I was ultimately good or bad. The answer came in the form of a memory.

I was taken back to my childhood and dealing with my first hurt. The way I dealt with that event, from beginning to end, was because I just wanted to be happy. All things that developed in me after that came from that initial response of just wanting to be happy.

I had done and chosen so many things in this pursuit of happiness. I had made mistakes, thinking they would lead to happiness. All my choices, both good and bad, were about wanting to be happy.

More often than not, I made choices that would make me momentarily happy, but in no time led to unhappiness. These pursuits—the selfish ones—were all wrong, and nearly all related to material things.

As soon as I realized this, I saw what was going on in the world. All people born on this Earth were doing exactly the same thing! They were chasing after happiness, and because of the way they went about it, finding only unhappiness. The only difference was in what they chose to find this happiness.

I realized the sad situation that every human was in because I realized how much grief I had given myself in the search for happiness. In my search I had made all the wrong choices, which brought on so many bad happenings.

As I began to develop an understanding, I felt so close to humanity. How much suffering there is due to this wrong way of thinking! I asked myself what the purpose of all this was. What reason is there for living?

There seemed to be no real reason to it all. I sat down and reflected on the question: "What purpose is there to this life?"

My awareness went to the pit of my stomach, the solar plexus, as I waited for the answer.

Normally, after being transported to a past event, the answer came from the back of my head. On this occasion, however, something very different happened. Something significant.

I went into meditation and suddenly had a vision.

IN THE VISION I was transformed into a butterfly. I sensed as a butterfly would sense. The world I perceived was the world a butterfly would perceive. I was flying through long grass and flowers. This state continued for some time, and was vivid and real. When I came out of it, my only thought was how strange the vision had been.

I asked why I had just experienced such a thing, but I received no answer at that time. I knew it had meant something special. But what?

Normally the answers that came to me were easily intelligible, but the butterfly vision only confused me. Every day, I would think about what it might mean.

One day, some time after the vision, I put myself back into the position of the butterfly and the answer just came to me.

The butterfly is life. It is full of color and beauty. It does its work, and it is just life.

At the time I was the butterfly, I had no thinking mind at all. I was aware only of my own life-force. This was why I had no idea what the answer was—because there was no thinking mind. I was one with the butterfly, and I *was* the butterfly. The thinking mind was gone. There was no distinction between what I was, and what the butterfly was. We were one. The butterfly was my brother. It was in me, and I was in it—not as mind, but as the life-force that was in both of us.

The thinking mind has developed out of evolutionary needs, but it is now over-developed and over-used. This has caused us to lose our god-like natures, and our oneness with all mankind and with the life-force.

It was then that I learned what God was, and what the devil was. God is the life-force, and the oneness of all life. The devil is the thinking, mechanical mind.

With this realization, I could figure out all the hidden meanings in the Bible. It is about the life-force—not the mind, but the simple awareness of your own being, your existence, and how it is identical with that of all beings in existence.

We are all brothers and sisters of this same life-force that, down through the centuries, has been called God.

I also learned that in pain was a gift of freedom, a higher self-love, and more than just self-love but also a love of divinity, a great love written across the heart.

This love was buried deep in my soul, and tied strongly to the emotional feeling center.

What good is there holding on to what is poison to the mind, body and soul? To continue to hold hatred for people who have wronged you harms only you.

Does anyone really deserve that?

The purpose of being pulled through the fire of pain is to become tempered, and so more useful and functional. Not forgiving means never passing the test, and never getting stronger.

Life is only a short stay, I concluded, and I realized my life would be wasted if I did not continue to go forward and learn. Every day that I continued to hate was another day not lived, a day wasted in an already short life.

And so I learned to let go. Let go of the hurt. Let go of the hate.

I discovered that the choices and mistakes of my life were a test, and that I could now use the lessons found in them to become a better soul.

Why let this chance go?

In my heart of hearts I knew all this to be true, and that the truth could set me free. The truth is already written in the great book of the self. In learning the language of the heart, and to know myself fully, there was a way out. First, I understood, and then I accepted, and then I let it all go.

The result was Freedom.

After practicing in this way for some time, I found a very significant change occurring, both within my reasoning in everyday situations, and perhaps more importantly, in the effects on my body and health.

At this time in my meditation practice I decided to add some physical training. The energy in me seemed to want to be released, though this was not a hyped-up, nervous energy any more. It was more like a healthy appetite to do useful things. It manifested in the form of a desire to exercise and strengthen myself.

I had still not achieved the transcendental state I had read about, and this now became my aim. One of the things that was holding me back was the simple fact that my body would become painful from holding one position for so long a time.

I found the more I practiced the easier it became to slow the thoughts right down, until for short spurts there would be no thoughts whatsoever arising in my mind. It was a bit like the difference between watching a monitor and seeing a straight line with no breaks, to watching one that has distinct breaks.

At this point I knew I was going to eventually succeed, and this gave me even more motivation.

A feeling of inner peace and calm was starting to become more usual during my daytime activities. Though that feeling was not constantly there, it was like a metaphor for the meditation. Instead of a one long, unbroken line on the screen it was slowly changing into a more broken-up line.

My ordinary thinking would be punctuated by feelings of inner peace and calm. I could sit in a corner on my own and be completely happy.

These were intermittent periods that seemed to come and go of their own accord. I did not appear to have any control over either their appearance or their disappearance. It was as if I had been given a Valium at times, such was the effect the peace now bestowed upon me.

I planned that, whenever these gaps in the flow of my thinking mind arose, I would hold on to them for as long as possible.

After much practice, the first effect that took place was losing awareness of my body. I was not aware I was sitting in meditation anymore. I would come out of it, and not remember where I was. It would take a short while to remember.

From the quiet gaps in my thinking, I would drift into a kind of dream state—but not sleep, as my head would not slump forward as it did when I fell asleep.

Then a new phenomenon started to take shape, and a new awareness formed inside my head. The only way I can describe it is this. Think of the working part of your mind, then from this, imagine that a new spirit-mind arises and stands next to your thinking mind. It is as if there is a new life-form standing next to your own thinking mind, but this new life is simply awareness. It is an observer, but at the same time it is you. It is quiet, and does not think in the way the thinking mind does, but merely observes.

Suddenly you find you have a two-dimensional mind: the thinking mind, and the one who observes the thinking mind in complete silence.

That is the real you.

From this point on, whenever you meditate this awareness develops and becomes stronger. As you continue with the task, and hold on to the gaps between thoughts, this awareness *becomes* you. During the gaps, instead of being in the thinking mind, you are now in a new location where there is only awareness.

That awareness has always been with you, but because of the strength of the thinking mind, it becomes submerged and goes unnoticed. We lose all perception of it ever being there. But this awareness is you.

With this awareness comes the knowledge that the thinking mind is not you. It is just a process necessary for your bodily survival in the material world. This is what the great teacher Jesus was talking about when he said: "What good is it to gain the world at the cost of your self?" (Luke 9:25). What he was saying is that the things in the material world you attach to will cause you to lose the real self, the real you.

This can be proven. Get to that point, and find out for yourself.

I CAME TO another point in my meditation. This particular point was normally reached after about two hours of meditation. A strong thought would enter my mind: "It is time to finish." It would completely take over the quietness and the slowly percolating thoughts.

At times, the thought about finishing came in the form of restlessness in my body, telling me to end the meditation. Once the desire to finish the meditation came, I would decide it was time to get up.

But I felt dissatisfied. It was my ambition to push for the trance state, but I was not attaining it. I realized I needed more self-discipline. I had to push past this point. So I decided that when this thought-pattern came back again, I would come up with a strategy to get past the block.

I had now begun my weight-training routine, and this gave me part of the discipline I needed to push past the block. I also applied my knowledge of the mind-body connection to help me surmount it. At first, when I came to the block there seemed to be no passing it. The wall was too high to climb. But as some of my life experiences had taught me, this was just my mind speaking. How do I know for sure, unless I actually pushed past it? If other people can do it, I told myself, then by all accounts it should be possible for me.

I did consider for a while the idea of body shape. Perhaps because of my body shape, it was more difficult for me than for others, and this was the reason I could not go any further. I countered that hypothesis with the memory of what I had thought that day on the quarry face. Similar thoughts had afflicted me then. My mind could so easily convince me I could not do something without my even attempting it.

I realized this was a bad thing to allow to take charge of my life. All this reasoning gave me the encouragement to set about the next task, which was to push right past the two-hour mark, and finally reach the trance state I had been so eager to achieve.

Another part of my discipline was to make sure that, instead of reading the Bible for however much time I felt I wanted to, I read for a set amount of time every day.

My whole day, then, was full of discipline. If I was not meditating, then I was reading the Bible. If I was not reading the Bible, then I was exercising. When I had a certain amount of time to be free from all things concerned with the discipline, I would let my mind wander.

Reading the Bible, plus the meditation, created an effect inside of me that was more than just peace of mind. Whenever I read the stories of Jesus's teaching and acts of love, it would open my heart, or as the spiritualists and Indian yogis would call it, my heart center. Though they say it is in the heart area, I always seem to feel it more in the solar plexus. When I felt it in the heart center, the feeling was so strong that it just seemed to dominate too much. It did not seem to feel as good as the feeling in the area of my solar plexus.

The stories of love in the Bible were a good way to evoke feelings of love. This had a very positive effect on the meditation and on how I felt after coming out of it. There seemed to be a strength in love that helped me keep me longer in the meditation.

Whenever I came to a point of unrest while meditating, and the thought would come that it was time to finish, I told myself to relax. I would examine every inch of my body and tell any area that was tense, due to discomfort and the like, to relax. The more I spoke to the body in this way, the easier it became.

I noticed that, when I did push past this point, the old feeling of claustrophobia would get its claws into me. I would start sweating, and feelings of fear would arise. But auto-suggestion, in time, got me past that, too.

I also noticed that the muscle system was tied to my mind in subtler ways than I had earlier realized. As soon as I told this or that thought to stop, I noticed the muscle to which the thought had been connected. As soon as the thought was gone, the related muscle would relax.

These thoughts were normally tied to anxieties which, under normal thinking circumstances, I did not recognize as anxiety. The way they tied up muscles in the body with tension showed me that they were, indeed, anxieties that had to be let go of. I did not realize till now how closely the mind and body were tied to each other.

Now I realized that the mind had a negative control in the tensions that it brought on in the muscular system. This, then, was what the block was.

I had gone down deeper into myself to find this fact. Now that I was aware of the cause of my failure to go further in the meditation, I could push past this supposed wall.

The gaps between thoughts had now became so wide that I became completely lost in the nothingness. At this point, I reached an endurance of four hours sitting in meditation. Though I say endurance, it was more of a pleasure, for I lost the thinking mind completely. The space that I had occupied in the meditation did not exist anymore. It was gone. I was gone. I had dissolved into space.

I understood now what it meant to say that I was one totally with the universe. I had heard this before, but it did not have the same meaning that I now found. I had become one with all things. I had become one with everything that existed, because I had become nothing.

First, I became nothing in mind. Then the body that I occupied dissolved into the space I occupied. There was no more body. The "I" was no more, and with this nothingness I blended into the "allness" of everything, of all emptiness, and of all space. The space that I occupied existed no more, as I was all space. I became bliss, total bliss. This was permanent, and this feeling was to stay with me.

The more I meditated, the more total it became. I did not want to come back, as if I went to back to the working faculties of my thinking mind, I thought this state might become tainted. The only reason I came back was to eat food to sustain my body. This was indeed heaven on Earth.

I had actually found the truth of what all religions spoke about, and what God was, and the meaning of it all. Through meditation I had reached the heavenly peace that religions speak about. This was true peace, not a half-understood idea that I had thought up or read out of some book.

I realized too that an "idea" is something others believed or found in religious teachings. This was not an idea. This was real. It was real, because I experienced it.

Though one may think that four-hour intervals are a long time, meditating for that long is the best thing that any human can ever experience. Time did not exist. Though I sat for four hours, it seemed as if only a moment had passed. This too was real, and not the concoction of my imagination.

Again, I say to anyone, find out for yourself! All you need to do is described in this book. You can experience the truth for yourself. This is the way, and your reward is bountiful. If you make the effort, you will prove to yourself that it is the most important thing that you ever do in your life for yourself, your family, and the world you live in.

If you choose not to investigate, putting forth your own effort leading to your own Freedom, then keep an open mind as you continue to sleep in a world you imagine is real. Perhaps your slumber is pleasant and has not yet become the nightmare that mine had, a nightmare so terrible that I eagerly sought my escape and found ultimate Freedom.

Remember this story. Should your slumber not remain peaceful, perhaps you will recall it, and let it also help you to wake up to true happiness and lasting Freedom.

❊ *9* ❊

Dreams

FINALLY I HAD accomplished what I set out to achieve. I had reached the state of consciousness called trance. Not only that, I had also read from the great book, the book of self. I had learned to know myself, and through this had become a self-realized human being.

This may sound like the ranting of a swollen ego. I can assure you it is not. Our great teacher of love and wisdom, Jesus Christ, put it like this: "You shall know them by their fruits" (Matthew 7:16). A bad tree bears bad fruit; a good tree bears good fruit.

The quality of my life changed dramatically. Finding out why I was the way I was, and why I reacted to things the way I did, changed me as a person. I knew all the tendencies in my mind, and the ways of reacting I had learned in my years in this body on the Earth plane.

One side-effect of knowing myself so thoroughly was that I also knew other people. I understood what made them say certain things at certain times. I saw behind their veils. Hidden motivations such as jealousy, hate, anger, love, greed, pride, empathy, sympathy, pride, need, want, and so on, were all as clear as daylight. I had learned to let go of all these things. After the work I had done on myself, made easier by the solitary environment, all my demons were defeated. Now, however, I could see the demons in others.

Another thing I noticed is that I had become a totally self-sufficient human being. I did not need external stimulation for gratification. All I needed were the bare necessities of life: food, water and a roof over my head. I did not need cigarettes, a woman or wife, a book, a television, or a gym. Though I did work out at the prison to release energy, I could have survived without it. Nor did I need to stimulate myself with pictures of nude women in magazines, or with fantasies of sexual encounters. The need to stimulate myself with thoughts associated with sex was behind me.

When I had first learned that my common-law wife, Jayne, had been cheating on me while I was in prison, I spent a lot of time in deep thought. Now I came to realize that my desire for sex had caused me so much grief and hardship over the years. I could see that this was the major cause of trouble in my life. Everything that was painful had been related to the sex-urge.

I could see, too, that people around me in prison were suffering because of this very same demon. After seeing the problems caused by sex-desire, I developed the strategy of consciously associating lust with a bad feeling in my stomach. Whenever I became aware of sexual thoughts or fantasies, I reminded myself of the bad feelings and experiences to which acting on sexual desires inevitably led. These bad feelings, I realized, were responsible for many of the predicaments I had created for myself over the years.

For example, whenever I had a sexual thought or fantasy, instead of letting it affect my body with the usual erection, I chose to remind myself of all the bad times I had with Jayne. I would think about the anger that raged in my mind as I held a shotgun to her head, or how I had to physically prevent her from smashing all the windows in the house, or how the neighbors became involved and then the police. I recollected the shame and embarrassment of having myself and my life put on public display for all the world to see.

This strategy proved highly effective for blocking the sexual thoughts or fantasies that tried to consume my mind. After some time, I reached a state where I no longer thought about sex for the rest of the time I was in prison. Compared to my prison colleagues, this was a considerable achievement.

I think sex-desire was the greatest devil of them all. I use "devil" as a metaphor, because that was how I felt about sex at that time. Thinking of it as a demon made it easier to do battle with it. I would never have suffered so much had I not had those desires. This strategy returned my ownership of my own mind and body. No one from the opposite sex could rule over me, because now I was the one who was in control.

I could remember as a young teen the very day I had first lost that feeling of control. It was at the time of puberty. Now I regained the sense of being in control. No longer did I need to bow down to sex-desire or anything related to it. I was the winner.

The prison had a library I was allowed to borrow books from. Quite often, the ones I chose turned out to be related to the teachings of the Bible. This was purely by chance, as I would select the books based solely on their titles.

One book in particular that I chose was called *Hell's Angel*. When I asked for it, I intended to give myself a break from reading all this religious stuff. The title led me to think this would be something different.

Hell's Angel turned out to have been written by a man named Brian Greenaway, who had been in serious trouble and as a result ended up in Dartmoor.

Dartmoor was where I was at the time I read the book. The author had taken a building course that I was also doing at the time I read his book, and it turned out that Brian Greenaway had the same tutor as I had. Not only this but he came from Gosport, where I was to be in a short while. And, by another coincidence, I would also have the same probation officer as him.

Hell's Angel was about Brian Greenaway's life, why he ended up in prison, and how he had become enlightened. These events had taken place some years before I was in Dartmoor.

Brian Greenaway became a Christian from having been a Hell's Angel. He underwent a total change of character in Dartmoor, experiencing exactly the same thing as I did in exactly the same place.

I felt the book had come my way for a reason. As time went by, this was to happen over and over again. A book would be directed my way to help me with whatever I was working on in my life at that particular time.

DURING THIS PERIOD, I was like the sun up in the sky. I did not need to take anything from outside of myself in order to have happiness and peace of mind. I could find these things within my own being. No external stimulation was necessary. I had peace, because peace was within me all the time. It *was* me. I experienced a love and compassion for all other beings the like of which I had never known in my life before.

In the past, I had quite rightly and honestly said that I did not know what love was. But now I knew what it was. My interpretation of love as a young man had not been far from the truth for most people. Love at that time was a need for the security of a particular way of life.

Now I knew what real love was. All life was precious to me, even the life of the smallest of insects. I could not even swat a fly. The compassion I felt was in total contrast to the state of mind I had been in when I entered prison. At that time, I had been totally cold.

The experience of "seeing the light" affected me on a physical level, too. Colors seemed brighter and more vivid. It was as if my physical eyes had also undergone a cleansing. My vision had improved.

I would notice small things which, in my old mode, I would have overlooked. Details radiated a beauty I had never noticed before.

When I looked at another human being, I felt total love in my heart toward them, with no prejudice as to their size, shape, skin color, temperament, character, morality, cleanliness, wealth, or anything. I just wanted to offer them my love without conditions.

I was aware that, although I had changed, other people had not. It was through my dealings in this world that I had arrived at my earlier character, the "bad ass." I knew that if I acted on my love toward other people, it would seem strange to the wardens and to the other prisoners.

To avoid this, I made myself into a lamb for slaughter. I allowed myself to be perceived as the person I had been before—the same way people had always perceived me. The difference was, I was now aware it was an act. Before I had forgotten it was just acting, and believed everything I thought, felt, or did was real.

Though I made a good job of concealing the transformation, on occasion my new being would slip out in one form or another. At times, others could plainly see that I had something special that most people did not have.

One of my newfound abilities was that I could interpret people's dreams. Another was that if the conversation ever turned philosophical, I had the answers people were looking for.

Some people were interested in what I had to say. The more I spoke, the more they listened. And the more they listened, the more they asked. It was events such as these that showed the external world that I had been given something special.

I also noticed that I would wake up in the mornings and remember all the dreams I had while I was asleep. Up until then, I believed I either did not have many dreams, or that I did not dream at all. Now it was different. Something changed that allowed me to remember what I would have found hard to remember before the meditation.

Not only was I able to remember the dreams, I could also control the outcome of the dream if I so wished. This was because through the meditation I had developed an awareness that stood beside my thinking mind.

The thinking mind, I discovered, is the precursor to the dreaming mind. These two parts are separate, but closely linked. The thinking mind is the result of effort, while the dreaming mind runs on its own without any effort.

Much of the time, we rarely use the thinking mind, unless we are working out a solution to a problem or taking in new data. The dreaming mind is the one that runs in mechanical mode. It just switches on like a television screen and plays on until it reaches the end.

Most people live in the dream state for a large part of their waking lives. For example, you can go shopping and pick up the usual groceries without thinking too much. Your mind is somewhere else. You do not have to think on it too hard, because you are so well-practiced at this act that you take your mind off to other places.

It is like being asleep. You have little control over the dreaming mind.

The meditation helped me develop an "observer" that was apart from the thinking mind.

Though I had cultivated the ability to observe the thinking mind in meditation, I found the ability to observe did not leave me when I got up from meditating. This awareness remained with me in my daily tasks as I interacted with other people or with my environment.

Sometime you hear people using the metaphor of an "actor" to describe this experience. It is as if you are just watching yourself taking part in some kind of play. In that state, you just cannot take things in life so seriously anymore, because you see everything in a new light.

I observed that if I said a certain word or sentence, a whole chain of reactions would occur automatically. Having repeatedly seen this,

I could see where things where leading before they got there. This increased my sense of being an actor in my own life-play.

Before I had been too tied up in what was going on and in trying to get things to go my way that I could not have seen this. Now, because I was this awareness rather than the thinking mind, I could be completely detached from any untoward or emotionally-driven reactions.

For example, before I might have perceived what someone said to me as an insult. This would hurt my feelings, or stimulate a negative response in my feeling center. Or perhaps someone might say something that stimulated a positive feeling in my emotional center and lifted my ego.

Now, in this new state, I found these kinds of events did not have any effect on me whatsoever. I was in a state of constant calm. It was as if up till now I had lived behind a wall that I had built up, and that whenever anyone was to throw something at this wall, it would stick to it like glue. Now it was if I had taken the wall down completely, and anything that was thrown at it would just sail straight through. There was nothing there any more for things to stick to. The ego had been annihilated.

During the day, I had a very well-organized routine. It was like clockwork. Every part of the day was the same. The only differences were in what people might say, or if I got letters, or maybe if I thought about certain things stimulated by reading the Bible.

When I was not sitting for the four-hour meditations or adding extra meditations to my day, an hour here, and an hour there, I was living very much in the world of my inner life. There was nothing that escaped the attention of my inner awareness.

In the outside life, I was more aware of how certain things may trigger this emotional center, but because this awareness was now with me all the time, I had learned to control many of the thoughts that were triggers. Being on my own, I had a lot of space to analyze anything that came up because of the awareness that was always present within me.

I had no control over what reactions other prisoners, prison wardens, or reading the Bible would evoke. But I was constantly aware of any of feelings aroused inside my feeling center. This would not have been not possible before, as I was always a "participant" and always lost in the thinking mind.

What I had learned about dreams was that if I had a day that evoked certain feelings in a certain order, when I went to sleep my feeling center would have recorded, as if on a video tape, the same feelings in the very same order.

Every night, the feelings would replay in my dreams just as I had experienced them through that day. The difference was the pictures in the dreams were not in fact what had happened to me. The dreams were just a symbolic representation of what was going on in my feeling center and were replaying these events of the day with different pictures of the actual events. Though the pictures were different, the feelings were exactly the same.

Appendix B gives some more information on how to use dream interpretation in your work of getting to know yourself.

❧ *10* ❧

The Material World

AFTER I HAD been in Dartmoor prison for a while, I met a man named Rob Row. We were talking one day, and I learned that he was from Gosport, the place where I was going to stay on my release from prison. Gosport was where Kaye lived, and we had planned that I was going to move in with her when I got out.

Rob and I became quite friendly, and I told him I was going to be moving to a place in Gosport called Alverstoke. He told me this was a well-to-do neighborhood, and seemed impressed by the fact I would be living there.

This did not matter to me whatsoever. All I was concerned about was that I was going to be living with the woman I had dreamed about before I ever went to prison. She just accepted me for what I was, and did not look at the reason why I was in prison.

It was only just before I was due to come out that I described to her the crime I had committed. But Kaye knew how to see a person's heart. If someone was full of shit she took a dislike to them. Evidently I passed muster.

One day, I was out on recreation hour. This is the time they let you out of the cell to watch television or exercise. Rob was in the room, and he seemed to have a blank expression on his face. I could see something heavy was weighing on his mind, so I asked him why he looked so down-hearted.

Rob went on to tell me he had a problem with his lungs, and that he had been for an x-ray. The x-ray showed there was something on his lungs that was not supposed to be there.

He had to have some further tests to determine what it was. I tried to talk to him in a way that would calm his mind, but I could see I was making no impression on him. My heart felt so deeply for him.

Being a man in one of the country's toughest prisons necessitated affecting a macho kind of bullshit behavior. This was a matter of self-preservation. There is an unwritten rule in prisons that you must never show anyone you are soft. In my heart, though, I wanted to put my arms around Rob. God forbid!

That night I went back to my cell and had a strong feeling that seemed to emanate from my stomach. This was a different kind of feeling from the one I had experienced in Cardiff prison. That feeling had been all about hatred, anger, and negativity. This was the other end of the pole. The only thing I could think is that it was love and compassion for a fellow human being who was suffering.

I sat in my usual lotus position, went into a deep meditation, and prayed also. I did this for about three nights, then left it at that to see if anything would come of it. I felt that the prayer and meditation were really strong. My focus was good.

Some time elapsed before I heard anything again about what had become of the matter. It must have been several months. Then, one day, I bumped into Rob out on the exercise yard. I asked how he was doing, and if everything was okay with his chest now.

He told me he had been for further tests and they found, unexpectedly, that the patch on his lungs had mysteriously disappeared without trace. It was as if he had never had it in the first place.

I was glad to hear this, and felt no need to tell him about my prayer experience. In any case, I was not too sure myself if my prayers had anything to do with it. Perhaps in truth they did, but I was being careful, because I had become aware that truth can sometimes be colored by bias. That bias can come from being worried about others' perceptions of you. Maybe you are afraid they will see you as an egotistical, full-of-shit person. Because we want people to think well of us, we shape ourselves to what we think is required. It is just another form of lying.

One day, I was sitting in my cell when I was summoned to go and see the prison governor. I had no idea what this was about. I had no thoughts really. I was just there, and nothing really mattered. I was not pulled in any direction in my thinking mind, because I had complete mastery over it.

Twelve months earlier, that would not have been the case. My mind would have been going in all sorts of directions, and I would have been nervous and apprehensive, and would have wondered if I had done something wrong. All those kind of thoughts might have been there, but now there was nothing. I felt good that my mind no longer had control over me.

Once in a while, the environment I inhabited necessitated acting in a certain way, and the awareness behind the thinking mind would give the mind a command to act appropriately. Within me, though, I did not take these acts seriously, and even found them laughable.

The prison officer came to collect me. As I walked into the governor's office, I sensed a light atmosphere in the room. I looked into the governor's face and saw a look suggesting he had something positive to give me. He even had a slight smile on his face as he returned my gaze.

He started quite slowly to say that I had been granted parole. A new and earlier date had been set for my release. At this, his slight smile became a great big smile, as if he believed he had given me something really valuable. He must have felt like Santa Claus.

Unfortunately for him, I could not give him the reward that he had expected by saying "thank you," or even by looking happy. It just meant I was getting out of prison earlier. There was nothing inside me—no happiness, no sadness, just nothing. This is where I was, right here in the now, and nowhere else. The future had not happened yet, and the past had already been.

Only in the untamed mind is there, to use Jesus' expression, a place of "wailing and gnashing of teeth." Memory should be used only to serve the function of survival; anything beyond that is an over-use of it, and a waste of your precious energy.

❧ *11* ❧

Out of Prison

N ow was the time of deliverance. I was out of prison and beginning a new phase in my life.

My first impression of the outside world was how strange it felt to see women as well as men, and having the freedom to walk around wherever I wanted to go. This must be how everyone feels having been institutionalized and then set free.

Still, this was not anything like the freedom I had found in meditation within those prison walls. I had made three attempts to escape, and succeeded on the third try. My final escape, however, was in a way that few will have the good fortune to understand.

What was my aim to be now, having been given this new life? One thing that enlightenment gave me was the understanding that if one is attached to an idea or an action, then from that come inevitable consequences.

In the religions of India they call this karma. In enlightenment, one learns to detach from worldly bondage. But all of us are dependent on teachings from each other, and learning never comes without difficult consequences. As the old saying has it, you have to stick your hand in the fire to understand that fire is painful. Our parents and books may tell us what is right and wrong, and perhaps for some the fear of the consequences will keep them in line, but for others, myself included, there is no fear. If one lacks fear, the only law that will be upheld is the law of experience, and the understanding that arises from those experiences.

Kaye and I had been writing to each other, and had decided to live together. It all just fell together. There was no planning or effort. It just happened.

It was funny how these events unfolded. So well did things come together that it seemed I was getting help from a higher source.

I went to stay with Kaye. The only clothes I owned were the clothes I stood in. She bought me some clothes on the little money that she, as a single mother, received from the Department of Social Security.

Kaye had had problems with her former husband, and it transpired that it would be better for them to separate. We were both at a time in our lives when we had experienced the worst of ourselves, and of what others can be, and we were both ready to create the perfect relationship.

After three years of learning to live with each other, that is precisely what we created. We blended with each other as a flower blends into the soil in which it grows. I was the soil, she was the flower, and she bloomed beautifully.

My purpose in life was fulfilled with her. What else could I do with my life? In the words of Solomon, "he who find a wife finds what is good" (Proverbs 18:22), and everything else is a "chasing after the wind" (Ecclesiastes 1:14).

Time flowed by, as it does when life is bliss. When one knows that all happiness as well as unhappiness come from mind, all one has to do is to call up bliss and make it real. Before I was calling up unhappiness; now I simply did the reverse.

When one knows Self, one also knows that the only sin is any act conceived to be sinful. If one lets go of the concept of sin, there is no sin. We are punishers of ourselves. We all have the right to freedom, but it is we ourselves who get in the way of our own freedom.

My newfound insight did result in one problem in my early years with Kaye. I could see everything about a person, and would instantly know where they were coming from, and what were the demons that possessed them.

Once, one of Kaye's friends was introduced to me. She was eager to meet me, since Kaye and Jenny (not her real name) told each other everything, right down to the most personal details.

When I was introduced to Jenny, the first thing I noticed were her eyes. She was full of curiosity as to who I was. She then fixed her eyes on the area between my legs as she and Kaye talked about domestic matters, and the things they wanted to buy for their respective houses.

I do not remember the details of their conversation. But I do remember that Jenny was full of the demons of lust and jealousy. She was in serious competition with Kaye. All she wanted was to have everything better than Kaye, and given half a chance she would have taken her man as well.

This was her main aim in life. It was all about material things, and she just wanted everything bigger and better than anyone else.

I could see all of this in the first five minutes. I had difficulty with this awareness. I did not want to associate with people who were like this. I had worked to rid myself of all these impurities, and knew there was a possibility of becoming contaminated by them again if I was not careful.

When I say "contamination," I do not mean contaminated in the way one catches an illness, but contaminated in the way of cause and effect. For example, when one knows the motivation of another is jealousy, then one has to deal with that jealousy. Having to deal with jealousy can disturb the peace of mind, even if one is not jealous oneself.

I understood that what had happened to me was a great thing,

143

but I also realized that "enlightenment" is not the last word. I had to learn to live in the world of people again, and have a method of protecting myself, otherwise enlightenment could become a curse. With the ability to see right through to the core of people's motives came the responsibility of finding a way to deal with this knowledge.

I meditated on this question, and came to the conclusion that, though I would not voluntarily want to share my life with such people, the consequences of my former life were still manifesting in my current life, and I had to accept that this life had to be shared.

Now that I was with Kaye, I had no right to deduct from her life. I was there to be an addition to her life—not a subtraction. From this point on, I learned to accept such things, and learned to be compassionate with everyone, no matter where they stood. I learned not to speak about what I could see, and how to pretend to be on the same level as whomever I was talking to.

There were opportunities of illuminating Jenny. When the time was right, I would use these to try to free her from her demons. However, it became evident that I could not help merely by using words. Though she would listen, she would not hear.

After she had given Kaye and myself some time to get to know each other, Jenny came round to our house quite often. She spoke very freely about the details of her own marriage. Jenny was a big lady and had a big personality to match.

After some time had gone by, the wall began to break down, and there came a certain closeness with her. I could feel for her in the same way I knew Kaye could feel for her. I eventually got to know her husband, Dev (again, not his real name).

Jenny told us she picked Dev up off the street as a tramp, and effectively brought him back to life again. He had spent time in psychiatric institutions, and had received all kinds of treatment to help him deal with "depression," or whatever label they had pinned on the problems in his thinking faculty. They even gave him electric shock therapy to destroy certain areas of the brain that they believed were connected to this depression.

One day, Jenny came over quite irate about an incident that had happened between her child and a neighbor's. Dev went down to see the father of the other child, and the father hit Dev in the ribs so hard that he ended up with fractures.

I had met Dev only once before, but had heard a lot of him from Jenny. My heart opened to him, but just as in prison I was not allowed to show this side of myself lest it be misinterpreted.

Though Dev was tall, he was skinny, and in the world out there he was a bit of a lamb against wolves. He was a target for anyone who wanted to be a big macho man, as is so customary in some parts of the UK.

I knew the value of a weight-training regime, so by now I had my own weights, bench, and accessories. They were mostly bought used, so had not cost a lot of money. I invited Dev to start training with me.

This was a way to help him. It was easy to see he was lacking in confidence and self-esteem, and if I could help him build up his body and put some weight on, this would go a long way to giving him something he needed to get by in life. Also, if he weight-trained with me, I would have an opportunity to talk to him and point him in the right direction in life, as I had answers to the questions most people want to know about life.

We started to train together. He was physically very weak, but as time went by, he gained weight and began to look like something. There were many problems along the way, but he kept at the training for a number of years and was enthusiastic about it. As I had hoped, it helped with his self-confidence. He even took up karate.

A NEW THOUGHT kept coming to mind. For some reason, I knew I had lived before, but I did not know who I had been in my last life. I felt sure that by meditating I would eventually find the answer. By now, I had come across the idea of age-regression through hypnosis.

If this can be done via hypnosis, then one should be able to do it through meditation, something at which I was quite accomplished. I had meditated all the time I was with Kaye, and I had been with her about three years by now.

I started to meditate, but arrived at nothing I could say was significant. But as I had already learned, nothing comes without persistence.

At this point I prayed as if I were speaking to God, and called on the name of Jesus. I knew it was about the strength of belief, and it was easy for me to believe that Jesus was real, even though I knew it did not matter whether he was or not. It was about how I could evoke the energy needed to make it happen.

Then, one day, I started to see vivid pictures of who I had been. I could see myself dressed in animal skins in dark colors wearing a hat much like a Russian would wear. I also could see myself living in a cave with two children. They too wore animal skins.

There was lots of snow. I was on my own with these children, without a wife, living in this cave. I asked why there was no wife to be seen, and it came to me that my wife had died. I left the life I had to go and live in a cave and raise the children.

I sat in silence much of the time, and earned a living trapping animals. I dug holes in the ground to trap them, and then skinned them and took them into the town, which was quite some distance from the cave.

Much of my time was spent contemplating the death of my wife. Inside, I too was dead. Day in and day out, I would sit in silent contemplation, or meditation if you like. I also remembered that the people of the village where I traded the skins would look at me in awe as if they took me for some kind of religious leader.

I would not make eye contact with anyone, nor speak to anyone, other than those I had to deal with for business purposes. I felt that the wife I had, the mother of the children I was raising, had some link with Russian royalty. I would sit for days and days in silence, pondering life.

One day, something happened, and I was given the truth. It happened much the same way as it did when I was in prison. I had found something, all the answers to my problems.

It was *me*, nothing else. There was nothing else at all except for *me*.

This was not selfishness. It was something else. I had found the eternal light! I had found the truth of my life and everyone else's.

I felt a great surge of love and peace. Finally, I was free from grieving. A new surge of energy came to me.

But what could I do, now that I had found all the answers to life?

Just live it! I was still young, and it would be a waste to keep this to myself. There was a strong urge to give all this to others who were interested in finding the truth.

So I decided to give it to the world. I gave my children to someone else to take care of, and paid for their care. The rest of that life was spent accomplishing that task—sharing the knowledge with others.

Though I could remember all of this, there were no names, and there was no evidence that could confirm the reality of what I had seen. How, then, could I prove it to myself? There was always the possibility that it could be a convincing creation of the imagination. I needed more proof.

So I went into meditation, and asked for proof. This was asked with a humble heart and a certainty that my request would be answered. I had a total belief that I was talking to someone who was listening to everything I was asking. The question was, how would I get an answer?

I expected it to come through pictures given to my mind. Perhaps there would be a way to get evidence in the real world and perhaps, with a little ground work, I would go and visit places if needs be to acquire information

I do not easily believe things solely on account of what is seen in meditation. There are many who can convince themselves of just about anything, and I did not want to make myself into someone like that. It would take me away from the truth I had found.

Some of the discussions I was having with Dev inevitably developed into spiritual discussions. I would tell him of my experiences to help him gain the depth of belief he needed.

As time goes by, people wear out and need something new. It is not that the truth is not coming forward, but it is the way of the mind. The mind has to have new stimulation. Though I had all the answers, he needed to find his own answers now, and they needed to come from some source other than his habitual mind.

One day during the period that my meditations centered on finding out who I was in my former life, Dev and I went to the library. I took Dev into the Christianity section because I saw value in the teachings of Jesus, and in love as something very important for a sound footing in life.

I urged Dev to take out one of the Christian books, but he said he had bad experience at the hands of a certain Christian institution, so I felt it was best not to press him. Perhaps something in the another area, such as Buddhism, might be more appropriate.

Dev was drawn to a book called *The Fourth Way* by P. D. Ouspensky, the one-time follower of Gurdjieff.

This was not what I wanted for Dev, because I thought it might be confusing not to have sound advice and teachings centered on love. I still thought of the teachings of the Bible as being the best thing for him.

Although I had found enlightenment, I was not well-read. Though I tried to put him off, he would not have it. He was determined to read that book, and so I left him to it. I hoped that one day he would, with a bit of convincing, take up the Bible, as I still saw him regularly for our training sessions.

Dev came along to the next training session, and talked to me about Ouspensky and Gurdjieff. I listened politely and tried to have discussions about the topics he raised. His interest was nearly always centered on these people. Though I did not know anything about them, I did not think that their teachings could possibly have any value compared with those in the Bible.

Then things started to happen that were extraordinary. The more I meditated on finding out who I had been, the more Dev seem to get possessed by Gurdjieff and Ouspensky. He recited ideas of Gurdjieff that corresponded exactly to my own understanding, and that I had previously believed to be unique to my own way of thinking

One day, he showed me pictures of Gurdjieff and some children who were supposedly his, though Gurdjieff had kept quiet about the matter of having children.

The children pictured were the very ones I had seen in my meditation, and they wore the animal skins I had seen.

As soon as I saw this, it began to dawn on me that Dev had been used by the energy I had called upon to help me find the answer to who I was. It seemed that the more he talked about this Gurdjieff, the more I recognized myself in the man he was talking about.

As time went by, there emerged much more evidence to convince me of this. I was born exactly six years, six months and fourteen days after Gurdjieff (or I) passed over from the last life.

When Ouspensky split from Gurdjieff, he said that Gurdjieff was going through a battle. One who can reach the highest level of development also has to, by the law of polarity, reach the lowest. He called it the battle between good and evil, and hoped that the good in Gurdjieff would win.

The time period from Gurdjieff's death to my birth indicated the numbers 66 and 77 (if we turn fourteen days into the seven-day cycle of the week). In some circles, the number 66 represents the devil and 77 signifies God—the battle of good and evil.

Another thing that emerged was that, before Gurdjieff died, he was close to John G. Bennett and Jeanne de Salzmann. He stated to both of them that someone was to come after him. Bennett thought that it was to be another spiritual teacher, though De Salzmann kept silent on this point. Though she was never quoted as giving an interpretation of Gurdjieff's announcement, sometimes silence can be an affirmation. Jeanne de Salzmann was the closest to Gurdjieff at the end of his life, and would have known his most intimate thoughts, even if she chose to keep quiet about them.

It was known that Bennett was a bright young man, and that Gurdjieff admired him. He saw him as someone who would carry on with his work after he died. In effect, Bennett did carry on, but went off into other directions, such as Subud. (Subud is a form of enlightenment that Bennett learned about after Gurdjieff's death.) Bennett also sent people to central Asia to search for the alleged Master from whom Gurdjieff received his knowledge.

Bennett founded a place in England, in Richmond upon Thames, to carry on the teachings of Gurdjieff. From one of his books, *The Dramatic Universe*, Dev read me a passage that involved a day on which something important was due to happen.

It was the day of my birth.

Not only this, but I was born in Kingston Hill, only a few miles from Bennett's institution. (Gurdjieff himself tried unsuccessfully to gain entry into the UK, but was not allowed.)

As time went by, even more evidence was to come my way about this past life of mine. During this time, my step-daughter had taken an interest in gymnastics. We thought this was a good thing for her, as she was very shy. It was an ideal opportunity for her to come out of herself.

Being a person who has interest in the art of the body in motion, it was not long before I too became interested in gymnastics. I could see how the body and mind could join together and become one. If an average, untrained person told his body to perform a movement requiring a high level of agility and flexibility, he might end up on the floor, tied in knots. However, a well-trained gymnast can make such a movement with ease.

Gymnastic exercises require a combination of dynamic movement, explosive power, and agility unparalleled in most other sports.

It was my interest in the ability of mind to command the body to accomplish feats of moving art, much as ballet dancer does, that drew me toward gymnastics. I even became a gymnastics instructor, and could be there at the classes my daughter was taking.

Sometimes we would arrange gymnastics demonstrations. On one occasion during the summer, we did a demonstration at the school my daughter attended. At the school fete, I noticed some martial artists were also there to demonstrate jujutsu.

I was immediately drawn to jujutsu. The movements themselves were impressive, but the people doing the jujutsu were an even stronger draw for me. I felt as if they were people I knew. Perhaps this was because I had always been interested in martial arts as well as boxing. Maybe I was just naturally drawn to this kind of sport, since it was also a contact sport.

The attraction, however, was not on the thinking level so much as a feeling in the pit of my stomach. Whenever I felt from this place, it was usually an indication that something with a deep significance was happening.

I concluded I must have met these people before, and that we had perhaps spent several life times together. This was my mind thinking, and in the mind one can think whatever one likes, since no one else will hear it. That is the advantage of having a mind to yourself: you can make whatever thoughts you choose there, without having to let others know.

After the demonstration, I walked away because I noticed a young lad with the group, and thought that if I expressed too much admiration for their skills, it might build up their egos. I was not there to build up my ego, or anyone else's.

I was putting away the gymnastics equipment when Tony, the sensei of the group, came up to me and introduced himself. I had seen him notice me in the crowd earlier on.

His eyes said a lot to me. He seemed drawn to me, and asked if I was interested in doing jujutsu. If I was, he told me, I could join up with them.

I told Tony I was busy doing other things, and that much of my time was spent on gymnastics coaching, so I did not think I would ever have time for jujutsu.

Despite the fact I said this, all the time that strong feeling in my stomach was telling me to join up with these people.

Some years passed, and by this time I had become a builder. I thought that building was a healthy form of livelihood, as it involved working outdoors and being physically active. It was a good fit for me.

I began my own business as a builder and prospered until a period when the whole economy went into recession. Work suddenly disappeared. One moment I had six months of work lined up, and within days it was all gone.

I found myself having to sign on for unemployment benefit. This is nothing unusual in the UK. Sometimes when we have spells of bad weather, builders and construction workers have to either find work indoors, or else get assistance from the government.

There was some misunderstanding between myself and the Department of Social Security. I do not remember the details, but it was a genuine misunderstanding. They thought I was claiming unemployment benefit and working at the same time, which was not in fact the case.

Because they were suspicious of me, they sent one of their inspectors to call at my home. The inspector they sent turned out to be Tony, the jujutsu sensei I had met several years earlier.

BY NOW I had another friend who was also interested in weight-training. He had problems in his life that he did not know how to deal with effectively. Whenever he had difficulties with his wife, he would go out and buy things, as a result of which he got deeper and deeper into debt. It was as though he was trying to comfort himself to relieve the sense of insecurity brought about by the troubles in his relationship.

His wife was also on this level, so both partners in that marriage created problems for each other by trying to make themselves feel better by buying things they could not afford. The debts in turn created even more insecurity, and the whole cycle started over.

I helped him as much as I could. We became good friends. I had all the answers he needed, though my answers were not necessarily the ones he wanted to hear.

This friend had also taken up the martial arts, and he would tell me about them. For him, though, the attraction was not the enrichment the martial arts bring to life. He just liked the image he thought being a martial arts expert gave him. It was the usual macho thing, where some men can feel good about themselves only if they think they are better than others in some way.

Though I could see this, I did not mention it. To me, we are all on the same level. There is no difference other than what the mind creates. When one knows this, one can become whatever one chooses. If I turned my mind toward it, I could be the greatest martial artist ever simply through the power of my own conviction. But you have to remember this is all illusion.

Still, I came to the decision to join the martial arts group, and went along with two friends.

As soon as I set eyes on the sensei and the group, I realized they were the very same people I had seen a few years earlier at the jujustu demonstration at the school. It was Tony's group!

In no time at all we started to get on really well. The sensei had chosen a group of us who were to do a special form of jujutsu he called Ronin.

The training was very hard, but I loved every minute of it. The doors would be closed to protect us from public view, and no one was allowed to teach outsiders the techniques we learned. Many times the going was so hard that I would have to vomit, but I still loved it.

I had always known that I knew these people before. A memory came back of spending many lifetimes together with them.

I could even remember the earliest of our lives together, when there was peace among men and no or few words. Dinosaurs had supposedly died out by the time man arrived, but I feel certain this was not so. One animal I remembered seeing stood on its hind legs and had hands that could grip in the same way as human hands. It out-ran humans, was much stronger and bigger, but was not so large that humans could escape it by crawling into caves.

It was because of this particular dinosaur that humans had to stop being islands unto themselves, as this beast was killing us at an alarming rate. We recognized that if we did not do something, we as a species would be destroyed.

It was the need to survive that motivated us to band together to protect ourselves from these beasts. In due course the beast was wiped out, and thus ended this nightmare for early man.

This also was a time when man knew everything, and was naturally enlightened from birth. He knew all things of his journey through the physical world and the world of the soul. He lived to an advanced age.

Then man made enemies with other men, and learned a complex system of communication. Man became war-like in order to possess land and feeding habitat.

To protect ourselves, groups such as the one I had been in began to study and learn the science of combat. In the early days, this was combat of man against man. We practiced together, and developed and perfected the skills of combat. As time went on, weapons came into use.

I mention all this merely to inform you of the progress through time of this particular group. Still, my experience suggests that the same things holds true for other groups of people who come together for a certain purpose. How can I be sure? The evidence of my last life as Gurdjieff proved it to me personally, and gives me the confidence to state what I have learned.

It is important for people to know that reincarnation is a fact. When man knows this for sure, as I do, then he will have to look at the life of this planet, how he lives, how he treats poor nations, how he treats terrorism, and so on. Though man will be quoted as saying we must make the planet safer for our children, he will be even more strongly motivated if he knows that it is also for his own future incarnations.

During my time in the jujutsu group, I became close friends with these people with whom I had lived in former lives. I told them this story, as they were also becoming more spiritually aware during this, their most recent incarnation. But where they had chosen not to remember their former incarnations, I had made a conscious effort not to forget. Though we were drawn together in different lives, I was the only one who knew for sure that we had all been together before.

MORE YEARS PASSED by and my wife died of cancer.

I had committed the worst sin, the one I had learned not to commit in prison. I had become attached to another human being. While it is true that I loved her, I also became attached. I had the choice to live in isolation, or to come and live with Kaye. I chose to live with Kaye.

Some three months after the passing of Kaye, I was at a particularly low point, and decided the best thing to do was to go out for a walk. I found myself going toward the town center, and was drawn to the library.

I picked up a book at random and opened it. On the page I recognized a picture of the man I had been in a former life.

It was Gurdjieff.

This reminded me of all the meditation, and was the final proof I needed of the reality of reincarnation, and my sense that I had come back with this same group of friends.

It reminded me, too, that the same thing would apply to Kaye. She also had been with me before, and we would eventually meet up again. Her passing was for a reason.

All this came to me now. I had been given fresh courage, and fresh motivation to live. It was now time to die to self, and to live so that the truth would get out there. I had allowed myself to suffer, because I had forgotten this truth. Now the ego had died with Kaye, and it was time to do good here on planet Earth, for the benefit of others.

This is a universal rule. You have to stop living for self if you want to be free from suffering.

Though I was never interested in buying books related to Gurdjieff, I felt there might be a need for them in the future, so that is what I decided to do. I bought as many books on Gurdjieff as I could, to see what additional proof might be available.

One book I bought during this period was the Gurdjieff biography by James Moore. Before reading any book, I always look at the pictures. As I opened the book, I saw three people I recognized instantly.

The first recognition was of me and how much I actually looked like Gurdjieff. Till then I had only seen Gurdjieff's photos in Dev's books, where he was an old man. Now as I saw pictures of him at younger age, I was convinced this was me. I felt as if I had seen this face many times in the mirror.

Another picture was the spitting image of Tony, the sensei, whom I already knew had been with me in former lives. It was a picture of De Salzmann.

There was just one problem. Though it was easy to see that Tony was De Salzmann, the problem was Tony's age. Though the resemblance was clear, Tony was already seven years old by the time De Salzmann died.

I was sure there was something I did not fully understand that should be considered in this. To clarify the matter, I asked many questions in my meditations. I almost doubted to the point of not pursuing it any further.

I could see the future, and found the more I meditated, the more I would see. Normally it was my own future. If I saw a world event, it came in the form of a news bulletin.

Since this was the case, the question I needed to ask again was:

What moves forwards in time? Whatever it was, it had ability to travel forward in time, and this could be an explanation. For example, about a year before her death, Kaye had a dream. In the dream, she saw herself dead. If she could see herself dead, how could she be dead?

I had been interested for some time in mediumship. Mediums have the ability to let the spirits of deceased speak through them. While delving more deeply into this phenomenon, I found that many of the thoughts I had were not of my own making. There were, in fact, communications from spirits. Before sitting in circles made me realized this, I had taken these thoughts to be my own.

From this, I learned it was possible that the spirit of another could enter my body and speak, even though I might think it was me. It was if I shared this body with other entities—if I made myself into a receptacle for them.

If this is possible, along with the ability of the soul to move forwards in time, it might be possible for one soul to live in two bodies at one time.

Hypnotist Michael Newton, author of *Journey of Souls* and *Destiny of Souls*, conducted research on age-regression. He regressed people back to the time before they entered their bodies—the period in between lives. His research supports the idea that a soul can live in two bodies, at two different locations, at the same time.

It is often stated that there is no time in the spirit world. Entering the spirit world is similar to entering an acorn and seeing the oak tree it will become, along with its past as a flower on the tree.

This must be the answer. It explained how Tony could exist as the current incarnation of De Salzmann, even though he was born seven years prior to De Salzmann's death.

Additionally, I concluded that the impact of former lives never leaves the personality once formed. Although false, these personalities are a form of energy that becomes spirit, and though shed to some extent, they are never entirely lost at the time of reincarnation. The essence, the feeling center, is what produces another body or incarnation.

The false personality, then, is much like a set of Russian dolls. Former lives remain within the psyche. If, for example, one was a warrior in a former life, then when a situation arises where one needs to defend or fight to live, the warrior comes to the front in the form of an aggressive attitude.

This idea also explains how mediums have what they call "guides," or "helpers," or angels. These could be their own former personalities, or they could be the spirits of others who have an affinity with them from former associations. This, then, was my conclusion about the matter of Tony and De Salzmann.

Epilogue

WHEN ONE IS self-realized, one has a complete understanding of the self. This means that one who has reached this point also has a complete understanding of dreams. Such is just one way to know a self-realized person. He knows the meaning of dreams, and he can control the outcome of dreams. The control he has of his mind in ordinary life extends into this control of the mind's dream life. He need not dream at all, for when he is in nothingness in the normal course of the day, then he is also in nothingness in the sleep cycle.

However, if the outside world impinges on his inner world by accident or design, then he recognizes the feelings created from the outside world in his inner life. By turning his awareness to the feelings he is experiencing from the outside, not in the mind but in the feeling center, one who is realized can see that they are two differing aspects of the same human being.

People who have not come to know the awareness located outside the mind believe only the mind, which is in fact illusion. They believe their thinking mind is their only awareness.

The thinking mind only imagines. When one becomes realized through certain practices, true awareness becomes separated from the thinking mind. This awareness is the true self.

The practice of watching thoughts arising in meditation provides an example of such a practice. At the beginning, one's awareness seems to consist only of thoughts. The thoughts are the person—or so the mind believes. But, with practice, patience and perseverance, one achieves moments of separation from the thoughts.

It is as if one stands back from the thoughts only for a short moment to begin with. Then one goes back into the mind and the world of thoughts. One's awareness falls back into the dream state of the ordinary mind.

If perseverance is maintained, much like a body builder, one gets stronger at holding the awareness outside of mind, and the awareness becomes apart from the mind. From this place, one can begin to unravel many of the questions of one's life. And in this same state, one can unravel the questions of others' lives, because this new awareness is separate from the personality-mind.

This new awareness knows that all the play of mind is just an illusion. The longer one keeps this awareness separate from the mind, the more one is likely to reach the state of complete bliss.

This bliss is all-knowing. It is not of mind, but is a feeling that permeates the entire body. It is total.

One knows the nature of all life, and of all beings. There are no distinctions between caterpillar and the human. Why not? Because there is only the bliss of the life-force that is felt throughout your body, without the division and labels given by the mind. One is part of the All.

The "All-ness" can also correctly be called "Nothingness." It is in the Nothingness that you find the feeling of bliss. It is also here that you find the connection with the Nothingness that is all around you, and also within you.

This Nothingness is also within and without all other sentient life forms. The feeling of this Nothingness permeates throughout the body to all universal aspects is called, in human terms, love, bliss, universal life-force.

That is why one reads in all the religions about the teaching of love and enlightenment. This is because it is just the One. It is this very same One that is in all beings. It is the life-force, and the life-force, as it is felt, can only be given the human terminology of love, bliss, enlightenment, God-realized, samadhi, nirvana, and so on.

If we go back to the question of why man cannot become part of this universal love or God-realization, it is because he does not yet know that it is his thinking that is the block that stops him from attaining this level of being.

That block is, then, his very own questioning, intellectualizing, challenging, labeling, and worshiping that which should not be worshiped. He looks for God in a man who is outside of himself, not realizing that he can find God only by looking inside of self. He wants to bend his knee in reverence to an image that is on the outside, without a clue that he has to go inside.

The very idea of bowing to one he *thinks* is higher up the scale than himself, and what he calls "master" or "God-realized," is the very reason he cannot attain such a thing. He cannot get out of mind, because he still labels and puts people and things on differing levels. He sees one as being better than himself, and another as being worse. He names one thing this, and he names another thing that. He replaces his ordinary life-ambitions with spiritual ambitions, not realizing that this is the very same situation he was in before.

Such a person has the right idea, but does not know the solution to his problem. He thinks that it is all on the outside, so he keeps falling into the same trap again and again. He loses one identity only to take on another, not realizing that the thing with which wants to identify is the very thing he has to lose.

This is evidence that awareness has not yet freed itself from the mind, because it is still in the mind. All the mind can do is to keep searching, but it is a blind search. It is searching for what it cannot see, and this can apply even in the matter of choosing a spiritual practice.

Imagine a deep, blue lake, and at the bottom of that lake is a treasure chest. In your hand you have the key to open the chest and win its treasures.

One person will dive into the water, and only go down so far. After simply getting wet, he comes back out and tells everyone he meets he knows all the answers.

This is like someone who joins a religion, but can not or will not go the full way. Because he has intellectual knowledge, he teaches what he knows, and can even be quite clever about it. But it is only what he has learned dogmatically in parrot fashion, or it is that he just loves the importance of his position within the religion. In truth, he only gives what he has, and that is very little.

Then there is the diver who jumps into the lake and, with great effort and not a care for his safety, reaches the bottom of the lake, uses the key to unlock the chest, and gets to the richness that is rightly his.

This is like the man who goes into religion to know the truth, and who wants to be free from suffering. He does not use the religion as a new means to create an identity. He is the one who will have everything he wants.

He has, by jumping into the water and going all the way, shown that he is willing to die for what he wants. And so he does, and from this death, as great Mother Nature will have it, he shall be reborn to the truth of himself and God.

To reach enlightenment, one must be truly motivated in the beginning. One must have much desire to attain this. It is at a point when one has had enough of life, one becomes depressed by life, and wants to commit suicide. This makes the motivation to find a solution much stronger. It is a positive, energizing force.

One might feel: "To hell with life," "to hell with everything," "nothing is worth living for." One becomes depressed by the situation they are in, and truly wants to die, as there is nothing in life that seems worthwhile.

At this point, one has already died in a certain way, because one has already committed suicide to the outside life. The control that the outside life once had is now gone. At that very moment you begin to become free.

From here, one must start the journey that leads ever inwards. This is the only way you can go. All the answers are within. One can only find the source of happiness within. The source of bliss comes from within, the source of God comes from within, and the source of all knowledge comes from within.

When I was in prison, this was much the way it went with my thinking mind, for I used the energy of depression to create the energy I needed to reach enlightenment, and to become self-realized.

❋ Appendix A ❋

Meditation

M ANY PEOPLE ARE on a search without knowing what they are actually searching for. The causes of this searching can be many. They may feel that something is missing in their lives. Feeling uneasiness inside causes them to look to the outside world to find that something they believe will ease that feeling—looking for something or someone they believe will fill the emptiness.

Some feel as if they do not belong, or do not fit into the society they are living in. They feel so different, out of place. People, especially in the West, move through the outside world trying to fulfill their needs. That is what they are used to doing, and that is what they will keep on doing until they become aware that there is another choice.

Most people do not even know that they have the possibility to move inwards to find all they need, and which is waiting to be found there. By moving outwards, all they will find are substitutes for the real thing that lies inward. Substitutes can ease the restlessness, uneasiness or dissatisfaction only for a short period of time. Then, other substitutes will be needed.

This is an never-ending process. The moment you realize that moving through the outside world is futile, and will not permanently ease whatever you feel inside, this will be the moment at which you make your first step on your path toward self-realization.

Meditation is a technique used to become self-realized. Meditation is not what actually produces enlightenment; it is a technique through which you become more and more aware, to the extent that you eventually arrive at enlightenment.

What I would like to show you here is that you can practice techniques or methods to bring you closer to your own source—to your true self. Everything that you do during your daily living can be used to bring you closer and closer to the source of peace and silence, the source of love and understanding that lies inside you.

Your true self is waiting in your center. It is already there. Nothing new has to be developed. You need only cultivate one thing on your path toward self, and that is awareness—not knowledge, but awareness. That is what will lead you to the source, to that which is.

You do not have to do anything other than become more and more aware. In your mediation period, and in your everyday life, just keep noticing:

How does the mind think?
What are you thinking . . . while the mind thinks?
Where are you?
How does the body feel?
What are you feeling . . . while the body feels?
Where are you?
How does the body speak?
What are you saying . . . while the body speaks?
Where are you?
How does the body move?
What are you doing . . . while the body moves?
Where are you?

You true awareness is "lost" in the mind. The awareness is the observer. You are the observer. To become aware, you have to take the awareness out of the mind—to go beyond mind.

Observe what the mind is doing, what the body is doing. All words spoken, all actions made, all feelings, and all thoughts must be observed.

Without identifying with anything or anyone, become the observer. You are the observer. The observer has no opinion, no judgement, and no attachment. These all come from the mind, and that is not who you are.

You are not all the personalities that you have built around you during your life. You are not who other people *think* you are, or want you to be. You are not your body, you are not your mind, your name, your religion, your job, your title, your gender—you are none of these.

Ninety-nine point nine-nine percent of the people walking this earth identify themselves with that which surrounds their true self, without ever realizing who they truly are. You are the energy that moves through your body and mind; you are not the body or the mind.

The body will die. The mind will die. You cannot die, because energy cannot die. It can move in and out, up and down, but it never disappears, and it cannot die.

The mind is able, through thoughts, to change this energy from positive into negative, and vica versa. Negative energy can and will cause all kind of moods, even illnesses. The moment you are able to live from your center, fully aware, no longer identifying with what you are not, positive energy will flow wherever you direct it, under your control, through the body and mind.

Then you will be able to participate in this world on your terms; you are in control of yourself. You are your own master, in your own universe.

Self-realization cannot be forced. It happens of its own accord. The more you want it, the further away it will be. Even the longing for self-realization will become an obstacle that will prevent you from reaching the self.

Forget about your want and need for self-realization, and forget completely that all comes from the mind. And by "forget," I do not mean suppress. Suppression will only work against your progress. See your wants, observe them, see your needs, and observe those too. Accepted them for what they are. Do not judge and do not condemn them. Do not judge others, either. Accept whatever comes up inside you.

It is in all of us. Greed, anger, lust, judgement, jealousy, whatever comes up, will be accepted through the understanding coming from your observation.

If anger comes up inside of you, do not identify yourself with the anger. Just observe how it feels. Observe from which part of the body the anger started flowing.

The situation or the person that created your reaction is only an object. Your mind caused the angry feelings inside of you; the object is of no importance. Focus on you.

Anger is created because of the way you use your mind. The moment anger came you were not at your center, you were not aware. If you had been, then no anger would have arisen. You would have been detached from all and everything. Nothing would have been able to make anger happen.

In full awareness, you can act in anger if you think it will have its purpose. Feel the anger inside your body; feel where the anger came from inside your body.

If you are not able to turn the energy that comes with the anger back to where it came from through observation, then express the anger, let it out, but keep observing the anger while you do so. Be aware of the path you walk.

If you look in the distance instead of looking at the path immediately in front of you, you will unknowingly stray off the path. You will not be able to see the path that leads you toward the destiny of your journey. You are looking at the faraway and so miss the obvious.

Only if you are able to observe each step you make at the moment you make that step will you arrive at your center. Then one day only the observer is left; everything else is fallen away. All that is left is emptiness, nothingness, you, awareness.

You have found all and everything. You will feel one with all around you. No longer will you experience division, separation, discrimination; all will be one.

You will be one with all.

❀ *Appendix B* ❀

Dream Interpretation

T o interpret dreams correctly, all you have to do is remember your dreams and the feelings they evoke, and then associate the feelings of the dream to your waking life.

To give some initial examples, I will use the symbols of a cigar, a knife and a gun. Freud believed these were all symbols of a sexual nature, but from the knowledge I have acquired, I would say that these symbols are not necessarily sexual, but should be seen in terms of the feelings connected with them. A symbol may mean one thing to one person, and something else to another, depending on how they associate the feeling center with that particular symbol in their daily lives.

If somebody is a cigar-smoker, and derives great pleasure from smoking a cigar in their daily life, and that person were to dream of smoking a cigar, this would be connected to the feeling center as pleasure. If we then learn that the person who dreamed of smoking a cigar was a religious person who considered smoking a cigar on the Sabbath to be sinful, it would mean the cigar was connected to the feeling center as guilt.

To connect the symbols to our daily lives, we have to feel where in our lives we can associate those same feelings.

Notice that the first part, feeling pleasure, is a self-stimulating pleasure done on his own in the quiet. But there is also a feeling of guilt about this activity. These feelings—pleasure combined with guilt—might, for example, be associated with masturbation.

On the other hand, if the person who dreams of smoking a cigar is a person who does not smoke cigars, who considers them highly offensive and bad for the health, and who would never do such a thing in reality, the symbol of the cigar means something different. Perhaps in their daily life they are doing something they dislike, and take no pleasure in doing whatsoever. Yet they are still compelled or drawn to do it for some reason. They are also aware that what they are doing could be damaging to their life.

This could be the dream of a gambler. He is spending too much money on gambling, but is compelled by his addiction. The day of the dream he may have visited a casino or a bookmaker and lost a lot of money. Hence, the dream about a compulsion to smoke, something offensive and damaging to his domestic situation. He felt the same feelings when he was gambling, but it was a picture of smoking a cigar that he saw in the dream. All the feelings were the same as those he experienced that day at the casino or bookies.

For both dreamers, then, the dream was a feeling-center replay.

Now we will look at the second example, the symbol of the knife. Suppose you dream of somebody chasing you with a knife, and you run away because you fear that when they catch you, they will stab you and you will die.

You are frightened of being caught, because you know that your life will come to an end if you get caught. Being chased and feeling frightened, means that there is something going on in your day-life that causes you to feel fear—the same fear you feel in your dream.

The person chasing you has a knife, and you fear that you are going to die if he catches you. In the dream, you make an effort to stay in front. You cannot allow yourself to slow down, because you will get caught, and your life will be finished. In the dream, you are in front all the time, and do not get caught.

This might mean there is something that you are doing in your daily life causing you to fear that your way of life will come to an end if you do not stay on top of things. The knife represents the end of your life in your feeling center. The running means that you fear losing this way of life, and you have to work hard to stay in front so that it does not end. The running is effort—labor—but it keeps you out of trouble.

This could represent a person living a life where they are constantly struggling to stay on top of debts. If they stop working, the way of life will come to an end, because the debt-collectors will catch them and take them to court.

The third example of a symbol is a gun. What do we see a gun as? What does it represent in your daily life? It represents a threat if someone is holding it to you. The threat concerns the end of your life. In the dream, this symbol represents a threat that can end a life—not necessarily your physical life, but the way you live your life. It means that something is going to come to an end. It is something in your daily life you have worried about prior to the dream. It is something you feel could change your life dramatically.

This dramatic change could be a marriage break-up on the horizon, or a change of a job, or something similar, but it is something that ends a way of life or living.

If, on the other hand, you are the one in the dream holding the gun, it represents power to change other peoples' lives. You could be an employer who has the power to fire people, for example.

A friend of mine, Mark Scott, has allowed me to use some of his dreams for this book, because quite often he has asked me to interpret them. Rather then keep his name confidential, I will with his permission use his correct name for verifiability.

Mark dreamed he was in a foreign country, a middle-Eastern

country such as Iraq. In the dream, he had killed the president of that country, was caught, and thrown into a room. In the room were people firing at a wall of wood. One part of the wall was brick, and he hid behind that wall, though they were still firing at the wall and hence at him.

That the dream begins in a middle-Eastern country suggest he feels he is in an alien environment in his waking life. Killing the president of that country means he ended something. The fact that it was a president, a male who holds a senior position, indicates possibly Mark's in-laws, or someone else in a position senior to him.

That he was caught and thrown into a room where people were firing at a wooden wall translates to whatever situation he feels unable to escape from it. The room is his mind. A room represents somewhere where you live in your mind and body. Had he dreamt of a house, that would represent the body, but because it is a room, it is the mind.

Firing at a wooden wall means that there is a part of his mind that is most vulnerable—a weak area that is easy to penetrate.

Hiding behind the part of the wall made of brick indicates he has made a decision to move from his weaker mental position to a more secure position, where he is not so vulnerable. The wall can be interpreted as a barrier that Mark has erected between himself and his in-laws, but because of the family ties, he cannot cut them out completely.

At the time Mark had this dream, he had fallen out with his in-laws, and said things to them that were very damaging. What he said was damaging to his mother in-law, hence the symbol of president in the dream. (A president represents someone in authority, or senior in the hierarchy).

That the president he killed was from a foreign country indicates she did not like what he had said. In essence, he had killed his relationship with her in his waking life.

This incident evolved from the loan of the in-laws' car. He went to see them once after the loan of the car, and his mother in-law gave him a lot of verbal abuse, which was symbolized in the dream as the firing of the bullets at him.

The room was his mind. The words she spoke were the bullets, and the holes were the hurt he felt from the words she directed at him.

After a couple more of these verbal attacks, he decided that he would not go there again, and thus he was hiding behind a wall in the dream.

The wooden wall reflects how he feels when at their place, and putting himself behind a brick wall is how he feels when in his own home, away from them. Because he feels more vulnerable at the in-laws' place, he dreamed of the wooden wall, while the brick wall of the dream, behind which he hides, indicates a more secure feeling, though he is still not able to entirely escape the firing of bullets.

He cannot escape entirely because his wife, their daughter, continues a relationship with her parents with visits and phone calls. He overheard the father-in-law on the phone speaking badly of him.

We have to remember these are all feelings he felt during the day, and his dreams represent a replay of what the feeling center experienced, but expressed with symbols.

Lightning Source UK Ltd.
Milton Keynes UK
UKOW052103170412

190928UK00001B/40/A